Number 134
Summer 2012

New Directions for Evaluation

Sandra Mathison
Editor-in-Chief

Evaluation Voices From Latin America

Saville Kushner
Emma Rotondo
Editors

EVALUATION VOICES FROM LATIN AMERICA
Saville Kushner, Emma Rotondo (eds.)
New Directions for Evaluation, no. 134
Sandra Mathison, Editor-in-Chief

Microfilm copies of issues and articles are available in 16mm and 35mm, as well as microfiche in 105mm, through University Microfilms Inc., 300 North Zeeb Road, Ann Arbor, MI 48106-1346.

New Directions for Evaluation is indexed in Education Research Complete (EBSCO), ERIC Database (Education Resources Information Center), Higher Education Abstracts (Claremont Graduate University), SCOPUS (Elsevier), Social Services Abstracts (CSA/CIG), Sociological Abstracts (CSA/CIG), and Worldwide Political Science Abstracts (CSA/CIG).

NEW DIRECTIONS FOR EVALUATION (ISSN 1097-6736, electronic ISSN 1534-875X) is part of The Jossey-Bass Education Series and is published quarterly by Wiley Subscription Services, Inc., A Wiley Company, at Jossey-Bass, One Montgomery Street, Suite 1200, San Francisco, CA 94104-4594.

SUBSCRIPTIONS cost $89 for U.S./Canada/Mexico; $113 international. For institutions, agencies, and libraries, $295 U.S.; $335 Canada/Mexico; $369 international. Prices subject to change.

EDITORIAL CORRESPONDENCE should be addressed to the Editor-in-Chief, Sandra Mathison, University of British Columbia, 2125 Main Mall, Vancouver, BC V6T 1Z4, Canada.

www.josseybass.com

NEW DIRECTIONS FOR EVALUATION

Sponsored by the American Evaluation Association

EDITOR-IN-CHIEF

Sandra Mathison   University of British Columbia

ASSOCIATE EDITORS

Saville Kushner   University of the West of England
Patrick McKnight   George Mason University
Patricia Rogers   Royal Melbourne Institute of Technology

EDITORIAL ADVISORY BOARD

Michael Bamberger   Independent consultant
Gail Barrington   Barrington Research Group Inc.
Nicole Bowman   Bowman Consulting
Huey Chen   University of Alabama at Birmingham
Lois-ellin Datta   Datta Analysis
Stewart I. Donaldson   Claremont Graduate University
Michael Duttweiler   Cornell University
Jody Fitzpatrick   University of Colorado at Denver
Gary Henry   University of North Carolina, Chapel Hill
Stafford Hood   Arizona State University
George Julnes   Utah State University
Jean King   University of Minnesota
Nancy Kingsbury   U.S. Government Accountability Office
Henry M. Levin   Teachers College, Columbia University
Laura Leviton   Robert Wood Johnson Foundation
Richard Light   Harvard University
Linda Mabry   Washington State University, Vancouver
Cheryl MacNeil   Sage College
Anna Madison   University of Massachusetts, Boston
Melvin M. Mark   The Pennsylvania State University
Donna Mertens   Gallaudet University
Rakesh Mohan   Idaho State Legislature
Michael Morris   University of New Haven
Rosalie T. Torres   Torres Consulting Group
Elizabeth Whitmore   Carleton University
Maria Defino Whitsett   Austin Independent School District
Bob Williams   Independent consultant
David B. Wilson   University of Maryland, College Park
Nancy C. Zajano   Learning Point Associates

Editorial Policy and Procedures

New Directions for Evaluation, a quarterly sourcebook, is an official publication of the American Evaluation Association. The journal publishes empirical, methodological, and theoretical works on all aspects of evaluation. A reflective approach to evaluation is an essential strand to be woven through every issue. The editors encourage issues that have one of three foci: (1) craft issues that present approaches, methods, or techniques that can be applied in evaluation practice, such as the use of templates, case studies, or survey research; (2) professional issues that present topics of import for the field of evaluation, such as utilization of evaluation or locus of evaluation capacity; (3) societal issues that draw out the implications of intellectual, social, or cultural developments for the field of evaluation, such as the women's movement, communitarianism, or multiculturalism. A wide range of substantive domains is appropriate for *New Directions for Evaluation;* however, the domains must be of interest to a large audience within the field of evaluation. We encourage a diversity of perspectives and experiences within each issue, as well as creative bridges between evaluation and other sectors of our collective lives.

The editors do not consider or publish unsolicited single manuscripts. Each issue of the journal is devoted to a single topic, with contributions solicited, organized, reviewed, and edited by a guest editor. Issues may take any of several forms, such as a series of related chapters, a debate, or a long article followed by brief critical commentaries. In all cases, the proposals must follow a specific format, which can be obtained from the editor-in-chief. These proposals are sent to members of the editorial board and to relevant substantive experts for peer review. The process may result in acceptance, a recommendation to revise and resubmit, or rejection. However, the editors are committed to working constructively with potential guest editors to help them develop acceptable proposals.

Sandra Mathison, Editor-in-Chief
University of British Columbia
2125 Main Mall
Vancouver, BC V6T 1Z4
CANADA
e-mail: nde@eval.org

CONTENTS

Editors' Notes

The evaluation of social programs in Latin America has evolved in parallel with a prevailing social discourse around the urgency to reduce disparities and inequalities. Latin America has the highest concentrations of income and some of the greatest disparities of all continents. Large swaths of population are of indigenous origin and they are frequently excluded from economic and political opportunities. Many of the region's countries are still in postconflict and postdictatorship stages, and the possibility of public knowledge feeding into citizen agency represents a recent entry into democratic possibilities. Evaluation, always and everywhere a significant element in the contest for democratic control, has a special significance on this continent.

But evaluation has also developed as a response to the growing complexity of burgeoning economies, geopolitical change, and a commitment to the social program as a means of governance and social change. The region as a whole has growth rates of around 5%, whereas countries like Brazil, Panama, and Peru currently experience economic growth of more than 6%. Along with this has come a breakdown in the Washington consensus and the emergence of governments more committed than previously to social investment and social programming in countries including Chile, Bolivia, Venezuela, Ecuador, Brazil, Uruguay, Peru, Nicaragua—some of these countries electing presidents from indigenous populations.

There is a widespread development of participatory or actor-oriented approaches, based on qualitative methodologies that find creative expressions with a particularly Latin American stamp (Anduaga, 2000; Geilfus, 1997). Participation as a concept was elicited by developments in the 1970s as a response to a discourse focused on an increase in production and productivity and the adoption of new technologies. It was argued that those living in poverty, including indigenous (original) peoples, had to be the focus of development, valuing their knowledge. The discourse was framed by thinkers and social leaders like the Brazilian Paulo Freire, whose pedagogical approach to community engagement sought to "politically conscientize" marginalized groups and provoke citizen agency. His thoughts, and those of the Colombian Orlando Fals Borda, massively influenced schooling and led to a uniquely Latin American approach to street-level action research (see Streck & Rodrigues Brandão, 2005).

Participatory approaches reached their peak in the 1980s in movements such as participatory rural assessment/rapid rural appraisal based on community-level self-evaluation (most closely reflected in the northern hemisphere in Robert Chambers' work and Fetterman's "Empowerment Evaluation"(Chambers, 2007; Fetterman & Wandersman, 2005), all designed

New Directions for Evaluation, no. 134, Summer 2012 © Wiley Periodicals, Inc., and the American Evaluation Association. Published online in Wiley Online Library (wileyonlinelibrary.com) • DOI: 10.1002/ev.20013 to ground development in community values and priorities (see Anduaga, 2000 for a review). By the 1990s these had been consolidated into an empowerment approach, strengthening capacities at community level for social decision making and the enhancement of social capital.

Of course, these developments are taking place at the same time as evaluation is becoming a prominent aspect of the work of international development agencies, most recently in pursuit of results-oriented evaluation, as well as the expansion of economics-oriented evaluation as a response to the desire for government for fiscal control. No less than anywhere else, Latin America balances evaluation practices in pursuit of the effectiveness and control of programs, with evaluation dedicated to enhancing public knowledge and citizen agency. Sometimes these come together, as in the case of Public Observatories in Ecuador (and elsewhere), which are semi-independent scrutiny bodies disseminating details of government policy, including fiscal policy, and feeding back the response of civil society to government. Nonetheless, a participatory thrust is characteristic of Latin America. This goes, too, for the field of economics where, for example, Manfred Max-Neef renounced his high-status economic identity to become a self-styled "Barefoot Economist," developing a theory of economics from village level up.

The development of evaluation as a discipline and a practice has been strengthened in the region since the mid-1990s (Chianka & Youker, 2004), as indicated by the following factors:

1. The creation of professional organizations of evaluation.
2. The spread of ideas and the use of professional evaluation in three key sectors of society—state, private, and philanthropic organizations.
3. The increase of evaluation publications.
4. A growth in evaluation training.

This issue of *New Directions for Evaluation* includes chapters by evaluators from Argentina, Brazil, Colombia, Chile, and Peru that illustrate some new directions taken on this continent and are grouped around the following ideas: strategic use of evaluation in public policies and active citizenship, innovative project evaluation examples, and evaluation capacity building and institutionalization.

Strategic Use of Evaluation in Public Policies and Active Citizenship

For some decades, as we have seen, Latin America has witnessed the emergence of new phenomena and actors who change the significance and the public value that people bring to social interaction. There is an emerging consensus on the need to recover the public sphere around a conception of a *citizenship of social rights.* As we have previously said, many of these societies are still in postconflict and postdictatorship stages of development in which the public/civic sphere has been a lost or contested site. In such a context, evaluation (the production of knowledge concerning public value) assumes potentially great significance.

Nerio Neirotti (Argentina) offers an analysis of the development of evaluation, both as an accountability instrument and as a source of social learning, through three distinct phases of geopolitical movement through which Latin America has passed. These phases move from paternalistic welfare statism; domination by the Washington consensus, and neoliberal policies toward the reduction of the state; and the most recent phase, which is the resurgence of civil society and what he calls "active politics."

Sergio Martinic (Chile) writes on evaluation and educational reform in Latin America, looking at both the methodological and theoretical issues in changing educational policy over a 25-year period, and the methodological response in evaluation. Also, Ludwig Guendel (Costa Rica—but also UNICEF/Bolivia) gives an account of conceptual and methodological approaches in his chapter on public evaluation, policies, and human rights. This concerns political, legal, and institutional recognition of the social subject, and an associated reconfiguration of economic and social policy, as well as of the administration of justice.

Alejandra Faúndez Meléndez (Chile) provides an analysis of the changing context for evaluation in respect of gender awareness, a key dimension of international development, and human rights, including those of indigenous and marginalized peoples. Her contribution falls within, and expands, the third phase of Neirotti's analysis—the resurgence of an active civil society.

Innovative Project Evaluation Examples

This issue of *NDE* gathers recent advances in the area of participatory evaluation of public policies, reporting studies made by nongovernmental organizations in Brazil. Daniel Braga Brandão, Rogério Renato Silva, and Renata Codas (Brazil) present an innovative evaluation involving the participation of youth as evaluators, with a methodology partly inspired by comic magazines. Ana Carolina Letichevsky and Thereza Penna Firme (Brazil) continue the participatory theme, presenting a community-based evaluation in a slum area.

Evaluation Capacity Building and Institutionalization

This issue includes two chapters concerned with the relationship between evaluation and public policy. Osvaldo Néstor Feinstein (Argentina), writing on evaluation as a learning tool, presents a conceptual framework showing the complementarity of the learning and accountability roles of evaluation. He addresses some of the main difficulties preventing evaluation from being used as a learning tool, suggesting practical ways to overcome them.

Nuria Cunill-Grau and Sonia M. Ospina address one of the complexities of the contemporary context for evaluation. Though Neirotti's analysis shows the re-emergence of progressive concerns with engaging civil society, Latin America is not immune from global governance trends and has embraced the new public management no less than other regions. This chapter looks at the institutionalization of evaluation in such a context and the tension between progressive, liberal aims in development and the control through accountability that attends it. And Rotondo shares lessons learned from evaluation capacity-building efforts undertaken by PREVAL in recent years.

An issue as slim as this can only offer a fragment, a small glimpse of a world of theory and practice. There is clearly a wide range across this enormous continent, and this issue cannot hope to be representative of it. Indeed, we have concentrated on those approaches to evaluation that are consciously part of a tradition of theorizing about evaluation in relation to public knowledge and democracy. This is appropriate to the main purpose of this issue, however, which is to suggest what is distinctive about evaluation in Latin America, or, better perhaps, what makes Latin America a distinctive context for the development of evaluation theorizing and practice.

References

Anduaga, J. (2000). *Manual of participatory and integral methods in the agrarian investigation for the alternative development.* San José, Costa Rica: IICA.

Blauert, J., & Pasteurt, K. (2001). *Participatory monitoring and evaluation in Latin America.* Sussex, United Kingdom: Sussex University, Institute of Development Studies.

Chambers, R. (2007). *Who counts? The quiet revolution of participation and numbers* (IDS Working Paper 296). Brighton, England: IDS.

Chianca, T., & Youker, B. (2004). Evaluation in Latin America and the Caribbean: General vision of the recent developments. *Journal of Multidisciplinary Evaluation.* Retrieved from http://evaluation.wmich.edu/jmde/[Spanish translation retrieved from www.preval.org]

Fetterman, D., & Wandersman, A. (2005). *Empowerment evaluation principles in practice.* New York, NY: The Guilford Press.

Geilfus, F. (1997). *80 tools for participatory development. Diagnosis, planning, monitoring and evaluation.* San José, Costa Rica: IICA.

Streck, D., & Rodrigues Brandão, C. (2005). Participatory action research in Latin America [Special issue]. *International Journal of Action Research, 1*(1). Retrieved from http://www.hampp-verlag.de/hampp_e-journals_IJAR.htm

Saville Kushner
Emma Rotondo
Editors

SAVILLE KUSHNER is professor of public evaluation at the University of Auckland, New Zealand. He served as regional M&E officer for UNICEF in Latin America and was president of the UK Evaluation Society.

EMMA ROTONDO is an anthropologist and executive director of the PREVAL Regional Evaluation and Systematization Capacity Building Platform in Latin America and the Caribbean based in Lima, Peru. She is also the founding member of EvalPeru and ReLAC.

NEW DIRECTIONS FOR EVALUATION • DOI: 10.1002/ev

Neirotti, N. (2012). Evaluation in Latin America: Paradigms and practices. In S. Kushner &
E. Rotondo (Eds.), *Evaluation voices from Latin America. New Directions for Evaluation,*
134, 7–16.

1

Evaluation in Latin America: Paradigms and Practices

Nerio Neirotti

Abstract

This chapter addresses the development of evaluation, as a practice and as a
field of knowledge, throughout Latin America in relation to the sociopolitical
context, including characteristics of the state and its relations with civil society.
It comes from the perspectives of evaluation as a learning tool, as a means to
improve accountability and transparency in public administration, and as a dia-
logic device. The political context is described in terms of three historical
moments: (a) the existence of the welfare state, (b) the withdrawal of the state
in the framework of the Washington consensus and the emergence of neoconser-
vative policies, and (c) the return of the state and the rise of civil society and
active politics. Finally, there is an analysis of opportunities and challenges fac-
ing contemporary policy evaluators and decision makers. ©Wiley Periodicals,
Inc., and the American Evaluation Association.

Resumen

En este capítulo se aborda el desarrollo de la evaluación, como práctica y como
campo de conocimiento, en toda América Latina en relación con el contexto
socio-político, incluidas las características del Estado y sus relaciones con la
sociedad civil. Se trata de la perspectiva de la evaluación como una herramienta
de aprendizaje, como un medio para mejorar la rendición de cuentas y la trans-
parencia en la administración pública, y como un dispositivo de diálogo. El

*contexto político se toma en función de tres momentos históricos: (a) la exis-
tencia del Estado de Bienestar, (b) la retirada del Estado en el marco del Con-
senso de Washington y la aparición de las políticas neoconservadoras, (c) el
retorno del Estado y el surgimiento de la sociedad civil y la política activa.
Finalmente, se hace un análisis de las oportunidades y desafíos que enfrentan
los evaluadores y tomadores de decisiones.* ©Wiley Periodicals, Inc., and the
American Evaluation Association.

Evaluation Perspective

To evaluate implies forming a judgment where the object being evaluated is
placed on a continuum: for example, more/less; a lot/a little; near/far;
good/bad; adequate/inadequate; achieved/unachieved. In every evaluation
there is a referent (a model, a situation, an expected or desired condition of
what is being evaluated) and a referred object (the object to be evaluated).
The challenge is to calculate the gap between the reality and the horizon
aimed at, and to explain the reasons for the gap. What is distinctive about
evaluation is that it deals with applied knowledge concerning public policy
decisions made in public spheres.

Every public policy is a hypothesis (or a set of hypotheses) of action of
the kind "intervention Y will lead to outcome X." However, the experimental nature of policy, especially in a globalized society, is subject to dynamic
processes of change that are both creative and innovative. Evaluation opens
up the relationship between the knowledge produced and the practice of
intervention, and is a powerful learning tool (Neirotti, 2008).

This learning leads to another function of evaluation, which is to
enable dialogue among those involved in the intervention, those we call
stakeholders, or those who invest value in the policy and the intervention.
Dialogue is focused on different calculations of value and diverse views of
the distance between accomplishment and the horizons of aspiration. This
is the 'deliberative' function of evaluation (House & Howe, 1999).

An evaluation must pursue two additional purposes in order to be useful. On the one hand, it must be an instrument to improve accountability
conditions, both internal and external to the program. Being evaluated
implies that agents of a policy can account for their productivity not only
in the statutory sector to which they belong (internal accountability), but
also in the context of broader political and social worlds (external accountability). The result ought to be greater transparency in social planning and
innovation feeding public debate about society's political heritage.

In terms of its methodological purposes, evaluation has a scientific–
technical dimension and a political one. The former refers to the rationality of the means with respect to its measurement purposes, whereas the latter is related to the interplay of power among stakeholders.

Technical rationality is not the only factor that drives decision-making
processes, nor is there only one scientific solution to any social problem.

Were this the case, we would find ourselves in the grip of technocratic and authoritarian regimes. Neither should the academic and scientific field settle on what counts as public value—this is a matter to be determined by the wider citizenry and democratic politics (Aguilar Villanueva, 1996; Merino & Cejudo, 2010;).

The Sociopolitical Context for Evaluation in Latin America

The development of the evaluation function in a nation or in a region has to be seen in relation to its own sociopolitical context. So it is important to identify trends in the development of nations, the forms in which the state works, the conditions of civil society and its relationship with the state as well as the shaping of public policy.

The practice of policy and program evaluation in Latin America can be characterized within three historical moments: (1) regulatory planning for development (called *desarrollista*, in Spanish), (2) reforms of the state demanded by the Washington consensus, and (3) the return of the state, the emergence of the civil society and contested politics. These three historical moments in the region correspond to (a) welfare statism—the period of the development of welfare states, prevailing until the 1970s and which was brought to an end by military–authoritarian governments; (b) authoritarian governments and the neoconservatives and the period of neoconservatism typical of the 1980s and the 1990s; (c) the contemporary progressive shift period entailing the rejuvenation of the state and open politics. To understand the development of evaluation policy and practice in Latin America it is helpful to elaborate what each of these three historical periods emphasized.

Welfare statism involved a determined intervention of an omnipresent state in social and economic policies and development planning across society. In general, it was supported by extensive political organization with nationalist overtones and the popular support of civil society organizations, especially trade unions, business organizations, and the third sector (Garretón, 2000).

Mostly through military intervention, authoritarian governments and the neoconservatives were designed to bring to an end advances in social rights represented by the welfare state and involved the minimization of the state. Once these welfare state governments ceased to exist, the scenario was open for the advance of neoconservative policies, both in economics (free market) as well as in state intervention (minimum presence, withdrawal, privatization, and outsourcing). The neoconservative turn produced a civil society, already beaten down by authoritarian governments, that was fractured and weak, even though citizen participation was encouraged as a form of competition with the state. State planning was withdrawn in favor of private initiatives following values promoted by the *Washington consensus*, a term that captures the economic policy prescriptions for Latin American countries perceived by the United States as being in crisis.

NEW DIRECTIONS FOR EVALUATION • DOI: 10.1002/ev

The progressive shift in the new century reintroduced progressive government in the Latin American region and a new configuration of political actors with significant levels of social mobilization. The state has recovered its role as a promoter of economic and social development and there was a return to social planning, though still with delegation of state functions to the private sector. There has been a remarkable increase in levels of organization and participation of civil society, but contrary to what occurred during the period of neoconservatism with a politicization of civil society. There has been a shift from competition between the state and the civil society to a relationship of collaboration and complementarity.

How did the evaluation function develop in these three stages? In the period of the welfare state, in relation to regulatory planning, important information sources were developed essential to the planning function (for example, for economic statistics, social census, and vital and educational statistics), though systematic program and policy evaluation was not carried out. Once big development-oriented plans were designed (a task driven by politics but considered technical), audits, follow-ups, and inspections were performed, and the emphasis was on the process only and the fulfillment of rules and procedures with little room for formative replanning (Matus, 1987). At most, evaluation was used as an activity prior to the implementation of projects and mainly centered on feasibility studies. The results, effects, and impacts of the policies and programs received little or no evaluation at all.

With the reforms of the Washington consensus there was a move toward formal evaluation of public policies. Together with denationalization, privatization, deregulation, and decentralization processes, and along with the creation of public administration agents, it was considered necessary to have evaluation agencies to monitor and assess the results of the application of the policies. The period saw the formation of structures for the systematic evaluation of state services, such as the National System for Results Evaluation of the Public Administration (*Sistema Nacional de Evaluación de Resultados de la Gestión Pública—SINERGIA*) in Colombia, the National System of Evaluation (*Sistema Nacional de Evaluación—SINE*) in Costa Rica, and the evaluation built into the Brazilian Pluriannual Action Plans at federal, state, and municipal levels.

During this period, the focus was on evaluation oriented to so-called second-generation reforms, with emphasis on the study of results and impact within the framework of the modernization of the state and the paradigm of the performative-based new public management (Norris & Kushner, 2007). The first-generation reforms refer to structural adjustments carried out by governments with the support of international organizations, mainly the World Bank and the Inter-American Development Bank, oriented to cut fiscal deficits and open up economies. Second-generation reforms were oriented to the transformation of the state and its health, education, labor, and social security sectors. Within this framework a deregulatory and coordinating approach was encouraged. More than abiding by rules, evaluation shifted its attention to the results, the scope of its aims and the quality of performance of the public administration (Cunill Grau & Ospina Bozzi, 2003; Saltzman, 2003). Under this new regime, the citizen is recast as client or consumer. Evaluation is focused on measuring user satisfaction with services through surveys and instruments such as citizen charters, but also focuses on monitoring the outsourcing of state functions.

The new public management was oriented toward the private sector and civil society organizations. These increased in number and level of expertise, though their participation was not significant enough to allow for the development of strategies, methodologies, and a culture of participatory evaluation. The bases for this kind of evaluation have emerged subsequently, but it will be necessary to wait until the new millennium in order to see the development of this evaluation style, in conjunction with the high levels of mobilization of social movements arising in the region (peasant, racial identity, gender, local movements, among others).

Notwithstanding the aforementioned, there was a growing demand for the professionalization of evaluation. Foundations of the institutionalization of evaluation were laid, the first concerns for the training of evaluators were raised, and support for evaluation research, training, updating, and professionalization of the activity was encouraged by government and international organizations.

Much of this evaluation development came not from national governments, but from international organizations. Evaluation activities were created in order to secure the effective development of proposals for harmonized action across the region. It is also worth noting that evaluation faced a dual purpose: on the one hand, to determine how public policies operated in general terms and in the institutions relevant to each sector (for example, provincial/state education and health systems, schools, hospitals, health centers, provincial/state and municipal social development offices) based on their results, but on the other hand, to encourage competition among different sectors in order to support quasimarkets and the exercise of consumer choice.

As a result of the increase in political mobilization, the consolidation of social movements, the development of civil society organizations, and the processes of state modernization, the region is currently facing the challenge of creating new evaluation approaches in the context of other public policy priorities. The presence of various actors participating in policy design and implementation is giving rise to a multilevel form of governance, where national government converges with provincial/state and municipal governments, as well as governance through partnership management, involving associations between governmental and nongovernmental agencies (Bañón & Carrillo, 1997; Bozeman, 1998).

These emphasize the political aspects of evaluation, where it is asked to strengthen policy determinations, to construct consensus, and to negotiate differences in values, interests, and discourses. Attention to the political aspects of evaluation has resulted in a greater incidence of mapping of actors; analysis of their proposals; and concerns for institutional, cultural, and identity aspects of the social groups involved in the evaluation. This has sometimes bent evaluation toward an illumination approach (Parlett & Hamilton, 1972) and an empowerment evaluation approach (Fetterman, 2007). Freire's (2008) strategy of considering knowledge a power resource has been rediscovered in the context of the "knowledge society."

One of the difficulties arising from earlier stages in the development of evaluation practice was that appropriate use of evaluation was deemed guaranteed by simply paying attention to technical aspects of evaluation. Focusing on the values and interests of the different actors at the inception of an evaluation, as we do now, calls for validation of the evaluation among stakeholders in order to secure consensus over the object to be evaluated and the way to conduct the process. According to Majone (1996), the academics (dominant among those working in evaluation) frequently forget that using data (or factual arguments) is not enough, and that it is also necessary to know how to argue and to persuade (House & Howe, 1999).

The contemporary use of evaluation is no longer considered the exclusive responsibility of decision makers, though it is assumed that the evaluator finishes his work when he submits the results of his research and the good use of such information will then be the politician's responsibility. But this raises the question as to whether evaluation systems should make their insights more widely available to stakeholders at all levels.

Results and Process

Movement through these three phases has produced a shift of evaluation focus from social planning processes to results—the former seeking to control methods of policy implementation through social planning and the latter assuming greater freedom in implementation strategy so long as desired outcomes are generated.

In a results framework little attention was placed on program process, avoiding causal explanations linking implementation strategy (and context) to results (Pawson & Tilley, 1997). Program implementation itself was a black box, and program managers were forced to use their intuition to match program management with desired outcomes. This represents a challenge for the current stage, where it is evident that there are no uniform guidelines for policy implementation.

Methodologies are emerging that respond to this challenge. Early evaluation provision under the welfare-state period saw the emergence of several organizations for the production of statistical information, and during the second stage strategies to survey results and impacts were devised.

A neopositivist evaluation approach was mostly pursued, and sometimes alternative, nonquantitative approaches were dismissed as nonscientific. Meanwhile, quantitative methodologies, mostly based on quasiexperimentation, generated little reliable understanding of the strengths and weaknesses of program achievements. In addition, information frequently arrived too late for decision making.

More responsive (and less costly) methods were developed, such as rapid appraisal, the use of purposeful sampling, before–after models without comparison groups, but also naturalistic approaches, which are characterized by their holistic reach and for including the perspectives of diverse actors. Evaluation became a forum for dialogue (Greene, 2001) and mediation (Guba & Lincoln, 1989; Shadish, Cook, & Leviton, 1991).

Table 1.1 summarizes the different parameters used for comparing the three sociopolitical moments and their relationship to the evaluation practice.

Opportunities and Challenges

As a resource for the improvement of public management and as an instrument for strengthening democracy (MacDonald & Kushner, 2004) evaluation offers opportunities and challenges to government and academic organizations as well as to civil society. First, there is a wide range of institutional evaluation systems in many countries, although these systems are largely sectoral and poorly articulated. Evaluation structures themselves cannot solve such deficiencies, though evaluation can highlight the dilemmas and shortcomings in infrastructure.

For several years, political agencies have been creating their own evaluation resources, and they have created a demand for professionalized evaluation skills in the region. These agencies have contributed to the mobilization of human resources from different disciplines (sociology, anthropology, economy, education, psychology, health, etc.) that are currently converging on the field of evaluation. This mobilization has given rise to a variety of opportunities in the academic world, such as master's degrees and other graduate programs or evaluation subjects in specialization careers. In addition, there are numerous networks, associations, seminars, and conferences focusing on salient areas (public policies, management, research methodologies, planning, among others) that include evaluation issues in their agendas for discussion and dissemination. There is a promising future ahead for the professionalization of the practice that combines the endeavors of government organizations, academic institutions, and evaluation societies or networks. In most countries, the past decade has seen national evaluation associations created at the initiative of organized civil society groups, and various regional networks of evaluators and evaluation associations have emerged. These include the Monitoring, Evaluation and Systematization Network in Latin America and the Caribbean (*Red de Seguimiento, Evaluación y Sistematización de América Latina y el Caribe—ReLAC*);

Table 1.1. Characteristics of Evaluation Within Different Sociopolitical Contexts

	State-centric	Neoconservative	State/Society Articulation
State presence	Welfare state	Withdrawal of the state	Return of the state
Social and political participation	National popular movement Politicized civil society	Empowerment of civil society (indifferent to political issues) Opposition state/civil society	Repoliticized civil society Political projects and reconfiguration of mobilized political subjects
Types of planning	Traditional and normative	Strategic with minimum state participation	Strategic with greater state participation
Rationale behind decision making	Preeminence of the technical and administrative rationale (planning and process control)	Preeminence of the technical rationale	Recovery of the political rationale articulated with the technical rationale
Evaluation system orientation	Production of statistical data to support planning	Systematic research focused on its validity (information production)	Focus placed not only on valid knowledge production, but also on the communication and use of that knowledge
Evaluation focus	Ex ante evaluation Audits and process control	Ex post evaluation Results	Results in relation to processes (management)
Methodologies	Procedure analysis Statistics Prospective (feasibility/viability)	Quantitative (impact analysis)	Quantitative/qualitative combination

the Evaluators Network of the United Nations for Latin America and the Caribbean (*Red de Evaluadores de Naciones Unidas para América Latina y el Caribe—EVALUN LAC*), the Latin American and Caribbean Monitoring and Evaluation Network (*Red Latinoamericana y del Caribe de Monitoreo y Evaluación—REDLACME*) and the Network of the Regional Platform for Evaluation Capacity Building in Latin America and the Caribbean (*Plataforma Regional de Desarrollo de Capacidades en Evaluación y Sistematización de América Latina y el Caribe—PREVAL*).

The relationship of evaluation to decision making is complex and depends on whether we think of evaluation of planning processes or of social budgets, the latter being more restricted (Cunill Grau & Ospina Bozzi, 2003; Zaltsman, 2004). Bringing decision making within the ambit of evaluation will go hand in hand with the growth of professional evaluation cultures. Creating the conditions for the proper use of knowledge produced by evaluation should be the work of the decision makers (to the extent that there is consensus regarding the benefit of evaluation findings), but also of evaluators themselves (by fostering dialogue, interpreting the demands for knowledge, arguing, and persuading) and of those in charge of policy implementation (those working in the production and distribution of services, who need to take possession of evaluation results).

Above all, it is necessary to convert the monster into an ally (Mokate, 2000), that is, to stop considering evaluation a threat (an instrument of control and coercion) and to perceive it as a democratic opportunity. In the short term, Latin American countries need to consider evaluation as a possibility to learn together by reflecting on practice, to use dialogue, to get to know each other, to recognize others as peers, to improve the quality of existing policies, to be accountable, and to make management more transparent and valued (CLAD, 2000). In the long term, we need to perceive evaluation as an instrument for deepening democracy, for creating enhanced conditions for equity, and for helping people to improve their quality of life.

References

Aguilar Villanueva, L. F. (Estudio Introductorio y Edición). (1996). *La hechura de las políticas públicas*. México D.F., México: Miguel A. Porrúa.

Bañón, R., & Carrillo, E. (Eds.). (1997). *La nueva administración pública*. Madrid, Spain: Alianza.

Bozeman, B. (Ed.). (1998). *La gestión pública. Su situación actual*. México D.F., México: CNCPAP/Fondo de Cultura Económica.

Centro Latinoamericano de Administración para el Desarrollo (CLAD). (2000). *La responsabilización en la nueva gestión pública Latinoamericana*. Buenos Aires, Argentina: CLAD/BID/EUDEBA.

Cunill Grau, N., & Ospina Bozzi, S. (Eds.). (2003). *Evaluación de resultados para una gestión pública moderna y democrática: Experiencias Latinoamericanas*. Caracas, Venezuela: CLAD/AECI/MAP/FIAPP.

Fetterman, D. M. (2007). Empowerment evaluation: Yesterday, today and tomorrow. *American Journal of Evaluation* 28(2), 179–198.

Freire, P. (2008). *Pedagogía del oprimido.* Buenos Aires, Argentina: Siglo XXI.
Garretón, M. (2000). *Política y sociedad entre dos épocas. América Latina en el cambio de siglo.* Rosario, Argentina: Homo Sapiens.
Greene, J. C. (2001). The relational and dialogic dimensions of program quality. In A. P. Benson, D. M. Hinn, & C. Lloyd (Eds.), *Vision of quality: How evaluators define, understand and represent program quality, Advances in Program Evaluation* (Vol. 7, pp. 57–71). Oxford, United Kingdom: Emerald Group Publishing Limited.
Guba, E., & Lincoln, Y. S. (1989). *Fourth generation evaluation.* Newbury Park, CA: Sage.
House, E., & Howe, K. (1999). *Values in evaluation and social research.* Thousand Oaks, CA: Sage.
MacDonald, B., & Kushner, S. I. (2004). Democratic evaluation. In S. Mathison (Ed.), *Encyclopedia of evaluation* (pp. 109–113). Thousand Oaks, CA: Sage.
Majone, G. (1996). *Evidencia, argumentación y persuasión en la formulación de políticas.* México D.F., México: FCE.
Matus, C. (1987). *Política, planificación y gobierno.* Caracas, Venezuela: ILPES/Fundación Altadir.
Merino, M., & Cejudo, G. M. (2010). *Problemas, decisiones y soluciones.* México D.F., México: FCE/CIDE.
Mokate, K. (2000). *Transformando el 'monstruo' en aliado: La evaluación como herramienta de la gerencia social.* Washington, DC: BID/INDES.
Neirotti, N. (2008). *De la experiencia escolar a las políticas públicas.* Buenos Aires, Argentina: IIPE UNESCO Sede Regional Bs. As.
Norris, N., & Kushner, S. (2007). The new public management and evaluation. In S. Kushner & N. Norris (Eds.), *Dilemmas of engagement: Evaluation and the new public management, Advances in Program Evaluation* (Vol. 10, pp. 1–16). Oxford, United Kingdom: Emerald Group Publishing Limited.
Parlett, M., & Hamilton, D. (1972). *Evaluation as illumination: A new approach to the study of innovatory programs* (Occasional Paper). Edinburgh, Scotland: University of Edinburgh, Centre for Research in the Educational Sciences.
Pawson, R., & Tilley, N. (1997). *Realistic evaluation.* London, England: Sage.
Shadish, W. R., Jr., Cook, T. D., & Leviton, L. C. (1991). *Foundations of program evaluation. Theories of practice.* Newbury Park, CA: Sage.
Zaltsman, A. (2004). La evaluación de resultados en el sector público Argentino: Un análisis a la luz de otras experiencias en América Latina. *Revista del CLAD Reforma y Democracia,* No. 29.

NERIO NEIROTTI is vice president of the National University of Lanús (UNLa— Universidad Nacional de Lanús), the former coordinator of evaluation programs of IIPE UNESCO, Buenos Aires Regional, and specializes in the analysis and evaluation of public policies.

Martinic, S. (2012). Emergent evaluation and educational reforms in Latin America. In
S: Kushner & E. Rotondo (Eds.), *Evaluation voices from Latin America. New Directions for
Evaluation, 134,* 17–28.

2

Emergent Evaluation and Educational Reforms in Latin America

Sergio Martinic

Abstract

*The aim of this chapter is to characterize educational reforms in Latin America
over the last 25 years, and the way they reflect the role, method, and use of evaluation processes. The main theoretical and methodological tensions that are created by the development of evaluations will be reviewed, concluding with the
identification of some of the challenges that are to be resolved in the future. Evaluation has followed educational reform through a number of cycles.* ©Wiley
Periodicals, Inc., and the American Evaluation Association.

Resumen

*El objetivo de este capítulo es caracterizar las reformas educativas en los últi-
mos 25 años, y la forma en que han resonado en el rol, el método, y el uso de los
procesos de evaluación. Son revisadas las principales tensiones teóricas y
metodológicas que se establecen por el desarrollo de las evaluaciones, para con-
cluir con la identificación de algunos de los retos para el futuro. La evaluación
ha seguido la reforma educativa a través de un número de ciclos, según indica el
artículo.* ©Wiley Periodicals, Inc., and the American Evaluation Association.

Educational evaluation has seen major development over the last 20
years in Latin America, similar to educational reforms seen in many
other countries. As elsewhere, educational change has been one of the

key drivers of evaluation development (Norris, 1990; House, 1993). Countries have understood that knowledge and information produced by educational evaluation is fundamental to account for certain achievements, understand problems, and design policies to improve educational processes and results (OECD, 2003).

Concern for the quality and equity of education underpinning educational reforms has widened those aspects of experience that are subject to evaluation; consequently methodological strategies have been diversified. Traditionally, educational evaluations have concentrated on curricular learning. Today, the quality of principals' management; pedagogical processes; teacher performance; and the use of materials, technology, and school texts, among others, are also being brought under evaluation scrutiny.

In Latin America educational reforms have decentered policy making with countries evolving toward decentralized and participatory decision-making systems. The region is experiencing a shift from a society that passively receives benefits to a more active one with a strong expression of its demands and with greater power to exert control over school-related decisions. All of these changes in society and the organization of educational systems have had repercussions for the development of evaluation, providing evaluation with a new function and forms of use.

Cycles of Reform and Evaluation

Global movements have driven contemporary educational reforms through a widespread commitment to social engineering cast as a modernist project (see Rizvi, 2009; Schwandt, 2009, who use the term *social imaginary* to capture the vision of a global value system and conceptual structure). In the industrialized West, these reforms have circled around the school improvement/effectiveness movement (Reynolds, 2010), emphasizing strength in curriculum and school control, robust external scrutiny of pedagogy, competition between schools, low-trust accountability, and an emphasis on educational outcomes. In the United States, this imaginary underpins the No Child Left Behind legislation.

Though some of this global "imaginary" is seen in Latin America, the progress of educational reform in the region has its own unique footprint. During the last 25 years, important educational reforms have been launched in Latin America.

Following Ozlak (1997, 1999) it is possible to recognize in these reforms three cycles, or generations of change. The first cycle, dominant during the 1980s, consists of institutional reforms oriented to reorganize the management, financing, and access to the school system. The second period of reforms, during the 1990s, was centered on procedures and results of educational systems. Lastly, the reforms of the third generation in the 2000s transformed the relationship between the state and schools and the ways educational processes are thought of, organized, and put into practice.

NEW DIRECTIONS FOR EVALUATION • DOI: 10.1002/ev

In each of these cycles it is possible to identify dominant paradigms in educational evaluation, and particular problems that are privileged by demands and requirements of the system.

Institutional reforms corresponding to the first generation of changes during the 1980s were directed toward the transformation of the structure of educational services. In the great majority of Latin American countries structural adjustments took place, all of which implied, among other aspects, the decentralization of services toward states, provinces, municipalities, and school institutions.

This represents an externalizing approach to reform, through which central governments transfer the management and administration of a great part of educational services to the private sector, as well as to states, provinces, and municipalities. In almost all countries of the region, this process was accompanied by a reduction of the public infrastructure and a rationalization of public resources. The main emphasis of these policies concentrates on the topics of accessibility and coverage of primary education, the improvement of efficiency, and the alignment of resources with policy priorities.

In the 1990s the reforms of the second generation were initiated. These have a movement opposite those of the first generation, as they are directed inward, that is to say, to managerial practices, the evaluation of the system, pedagogical procedures, and the cultural content transmitted in schools through curriculum.

In this phase, policies that give more autonomy and power to principals were promoted; changes at the curriculum level were implemented, as were changes that concern the initial training of teachers. It is a period of important investments in infrastructure, including the provision of textbooks and other assets for the poorest schools in the countries of Latin America.

Nowadays, the signs of a third cycle can be appreciated, as the relations between school and society are redefined. The changes of the third generation point to more autonomous educational units, but operating in interconnected networks. This has put more emphasis on the quality of results rather than on the strategies or paths to achieve them. It is defined by accountability and the use of authority to enforce it. Table 2.1 summarizes the characteristics of these movements of reform.

These cycles do not occur in a simple linear fashion and are experienced in distinct ways in different countries. Each of these movements of reform is also characterized by particular preoccupations with evaluation, all of which are approached from the theoretical and methodological developments of their own time.

The first generation of reforms is centered on what the system offers and on the efficiency of its functioning. It is a period during which an economical approach predominates, and is directed towards the study of costs and benefits of actions taken. A great part of evaluation concentrates on the

Table 2.1. Cycles of Reforms in Latin America

	Cycles		
	1980s	1990s	2000s
Control	Resources	Curriculum	Results
Key actor	Private sector/ municipalities/ provinces	State/universities	Schools/citizens
Main policy	Decentralization	Curricular change	Quality/ regulation
Key processes	Management	Classroom interaction	Accountability
School decisions	Dependent	Counseled	Autonomous
Curriculum based on	Information	Knowledge	Skills
Pedagogy	Directive	Directive–flexible	Flexible
Teacher	Employee/ dependent	Professional/ regulated	Professional/ autonomous
Evaluation	Efficiency	Absolute learning	Relative learning
Measurement based on	Norms	Criteria	Standards

efficiency of the educational system, and learning assessments are made, predominantly, based on *norms* that organize the population in relation to the average and percentage of correct answers. At the same time, it is a period for the design and organization of national systems of evaluation (see Wolf, 2006).

In the second generation of reforms, an important element of studies concentrates on learning results and associated factors that may explain them. Evaluation aims to demonstrate learning outcomes and associated explanatory variables. A form of learning assessment is initiated based on *criteria* related to the achievement of knowledge, skills, and abilities. The focus is on schools and the diverse factors associated with their results. Studies of effective schools are conducted, as well as observation and evaluation of pedagogical practices and school leadership, among others. During this phase, national evaluation systems are consolidated; some countries of the region participate in international tests such as the TIMSS or the PISA, and the Latin American Laboratory for the Evaluation of Educational Quality (LLECE, in Spanish) is organized and sponsored by UNESCO's Regional Office.

In the third generation of reforms, the emphasis is on results and accountability issues. This is a period of great methodological challenges for investigation and the systems oriented to the use of information. The quality of educational results continues to be the focus of concern, but, at the same time, the study of pedagogical procedures and context-related learning in different social and cultural scenarios for students stand out as topics of interest.

It is a period during which new theoretical models and methodological tools acquire importance, and allow the evaluation of progress with student's achievements and the added value of the school they are in. *Added value* examines results in relation to a school population, meaning that, instead of comparing the average of one establishment with that of another, what is compared is the progress of any given student and the educational establishment he/she is in, with an initial measurement value and its projection. The comparison is with oneself (Ravela, 2001). In Argentina, Brazil, Chile, and Uruguay, for example, important advances can be observed in this direction.

On the other hand, this latest generation of reforms has a broader concept of educational quality, posing methodological challenges concerned with the object of study and the instruments of evaluation to be used. Learning is assumed to be cognitive, ethical, and social; it occurs throughout the course of life and depends on multivariate factors. What stands out is the necessity to evaluate the quality of action inside the classroom, the performance of teachers, and the work of school leadership.

Changes in Evaluation Paradigms

At the same time, shifting generations of reform coincide with changes in theories and methodological developments of evaluation in general. Current theories surpass social, biological, and cultural determinisms that characterized a greater part of the evaluations of the preceding 20 years or more. Today, evaluation is conducted on the basis of more complex models, and explanations are sought within the internal procedures of schools, pedagogical practices and the subjectivities of the actors involved (Shepard, 2000; Tylor & Lyons, 1996).

The major part of evaluation falls within a positivist tradition; it has measured the fulfillment of objectives and privileges experimental design above alternative approaches. These studies have also demonstrated the importance of social context as an explanatory factor for learning results.

In many evaluations undertaken in Latin America, social variables and the cultural capital of families are the main factors considered in the explanation of learning problems. Schools reproduce social inequities that originate in social structure, and the factors associated with learning processes inside the school remain in a black box (Buendía et al., 2004; Ravela et al., 2000).

Faced with this paradigm, a different theory was developed in the region, which consolidated itself near the end of the 1980s. In Latin America the works of Schiefelbein and Farrel (1975) demonstrate, contrary to Coleman (1966) in the United States, that in the case of the poorest countries, schooling *does make a difference* and has greater impact, compared to more developed societies. Primary schools, they argue, are more effective given that acquisition of knowledge depends more on school than on socialization and family culture. This realization gave rise to a questioning of structuralist paradigms of investigation and the development of evaluation centered on the school's contribution through pedagogical interactions.

At the end of the 1990s these kinds of studies were influenced by the effective school movement coming from more developed countries (Creemers, 1994; Reynolds, 2010; Slavin, 1996). The claim was that an effective school is one in which students reach quality educational goals independent of their social origin. These studies emphasize the procedures and factors associated with learning in relation to school culture and pedagogical practices.

Investigations conducted in Latin America provide evidence for the idea that, once social and cultural variables associated with children's families are controlled, learning depends primarily on the quality of the interactions and pedagogical processes inside school (Martinic, 2003; Murillo, 2003, 2004, 2005, 2007). This perspective poses enormous challenges for evaluative investigation, in the sense that it demands the construction of complex analytic models that need to consider the social context and internal processes of schools, hence the internal perspective of this second generation.

School effectiveness studies identify five key variables in the black box (i.e., the curriculum process) that are related to desired learning outcomes, and reflect much of the global imaginary mentioned earlier. These are strong educational leadership, high expectations concerned with the students' academic results, emphasis on basic skills, a secure and disciplined climate, and frequent evaluations of the students' progress (Edmonds, 1979; Reynolds, 2010).

These variables do not necessarily translate to contexts in Latin America. Therefore, a strong challenge to the adaptation and validation of new models exists in the region. For example, metareviews demonstrate that, in contexts characterized by poverty, factors associated with learning quality are objectives aiming at the students' learning, affective and effective pedagogical practices, parent participation, support to teachers' professional development, directive teamwork, and high expectations of students' actual learning (Martinic, 2003; Muijs, 2003; Raczynski & Muñoz, 2005; Sandoval & Barrón, 2007; Zorrilla & Ruíz, 2007).

In summary, in the last three decades an interesting evolution of evaluative studies can be observed in Latin America that shift from analysis of external factors to giving greater importance to internal processes, including the interactions and subjectivities of the actors inside schools and classroom contexts. It is precisely on these types of interactions that the possibility of change and improvement in school rests, notwithstanding contextual factors that impose unequal life conditions on children.

Changes in Methodology and Instruments

From a methodological point of view, these changes are translated into the design of more complex models of analysis. Multilevel evaluation has been developed and many studies are starting to work with mixed designs, integrating different strategies and techniques, both quantitative and qualitative. Furthermore, an interesting discussion has arisen over the quality of evaluation tests and their effects on the educational system. Among critiques of educational evaluation, the following stand out: tests measure learning as acquired knowledge and not as a skill or degree of performance; reasoning and problem-solving skills are not evaluated; and communicative abilities, oral and written, are not considered (Pini, 2000; Ravela, Wolf, Valverde, & Esquivel, 2006). Furthermore, it has been confirmed that national multiple choice tests simplify the curriculum as teachers begin to teach to the test (Darling-Hammond, 2004; Ravela, 2001).

Lastly, and this is one of the most complex consequences inside the region, the publication of test results penalizes schools that score poorly. This produces a tendency toward selection of elite students and encouraging parents to abandon or change underperforming schools, all with the purpose of raising the average scores. In order to overcome these problems, it is important to make changes in the constructs and the development of tests that permit the assessment of learning based on different levels of student achievement (Baker & Linn, 2002; Darling-Hammond, 2004; Ravitch, 1996). To confront negative consequences of the use of tests that have important repercussions on the system, it becomes imperative to develop evaluation that accounts for the progress of learning and controls for contextual factors associated with students' social realities.

Apart from advances made in learning theories, there exists a wide consensus over the fact that the evaluation of a quality education must not be centered exclusively on the students' cognitive learning. For UNESCO, for example, quality education does not only involve "learning to know," but is also "learning to live together." There is no doubt that a quality education is able to achieve a proper synthesis between the learning of certain content and the development of those areas already mentioned. This concept poses methodological challenges for the evaluation of other areas and dimensions of child development. It is necessary to evaluate not only results, but educational processes as well. In effect, quality must consider learning and other factors that may account for the effectiveness of educational processes developed within the establishments, which lead to better learning.

The widening of the focus and object of evaluation implicates other instruments that permit, for example, the assessment of teachers' and administrators' performance, classroom practices, and the school as an institution.

NEW DIRECTIONS FOR EVALUATION • DOI: 10.1002/ev

At the same time, it becomes necessary that these measures pick up quantitative and qualitative information in order to account for school culture in all its complexity. Indeed, the concerns favor new relationships between quantitative and qualitative methods (Stake, 2004).

Quantitative methods have come to be applied with greater complexity in line with the assumption that variables do not behave in a linear and commutative form, but in dynamic relationships, like a network of interrelations between several factors in a given context. In the 1990s, such an approach led to the application of new statistical procedures based on hierarchical linear models and the design of more comprehensive analytical models.

For its own part, qualitative evaluation in Latin America has also reached an important stage of progress. Various studies have demonstrated the importance of representations, the interactions and cultural contexts in which pedagogical practices take place, and of innovation policies and programs. It has been established that variables such as school culture, the expectations teachers have about their students, and the internal overall climate constitute crucial factors that affect learning quality (Carlson, 2000; Martinic, 2003; Muijs, 2003; UNICEF, 2005). The development of ethnographic approaches, the analysis of discourse inside the classroom, and the use of video records as a form of record have favored comparisons and qualitative studies concerning teaching processes and classroom procedures in different cultural contexts (Candela, 1995; Ezpeleta & Weiss, 2000; Rockwell, 1995).

The Use of Evaluation Results

The implementation of evaluation systems assumes that once results are known, these will be widely employed by their users in different decision fields. The underlying theory of action is that information produces changes in the subjects' practices. From this perspective, the majority of evaluation systems are organized with the purpose of providing information to, at least, four groups of people who require it for making decisions: authorities, leaders, educators, and families.

Traditionally, the main recipients for the information provided by evaluation have been authorities and higher administrators inside Education Ministries. It is assumed that they are the ones who make decisions or counsel the people who take them, so they must have the best information possible. This approach takes for granted that decisions rest on objective and rational forms of argumentation. In this sense, the more information and empirical evidence there is, the better the decision. Evaluation is defined as the basis of a rational decision and is further conceived as a neutral and objective activity that is beyond particular interests (reflecting the Schwandt, 2009, characterization of the Western evaluation imaginary as a Modernist project).

NEW DIRECTIONS FOR EVALUATION • DOI: 10.1002/ev

Most evaluative studies in the region have answered these kinds of needs. Nevertheless, their impact on decisions taken has been less than expected. Decisions are often made before the investigations are concluded, under pressure and preferences from influential interest groups. At the same time, decisions or the strength of the advice provided are not always located at the top of a system, but also at the base, and are related to the involvement of interest groups inside civil society over the definition and discussion of the public agenda.

At another level of the system, rational information theory suggests that data gathered by evaluations are important for school leaders and educators to produce changes in their working procedures and in the quality of results. However, it has been demonstrated that evaluations are narrowly used by school leaders and teachers, and have a minimal effect on their practices. In Chile, for example, national evaluation results are not utilized by principals and educators and have little consequence for changes in teaching and learning matters. As for parents, information is not communicated in a way that makes changes and results transparent or understandable. The communication of evaluation findings presupposes capacities that are not always present in many families, including reading comprehension skills, the knowledge of key mathematical concepts (average, percentage), and the ability to read tables and graphs (Ravela et al., 2006).

On the whole, despite abundant information and the development of evaluation systems, there are deficiencies in communication with actors involved, and interpretations that may help them understand educational issues are missing. The way results are communicated does not generally consider the languages and realities of diverse actors in educational communities.

Conclusions

Cycles of educational reform have influenced the conceptions and status of educational evaluation in Latin America, which coincide with changes in theories and methodologies of evaluation. As new problems emerge, so do strategies to deal with them.

Over the last two decades there have been changes in theories and methods used for educational evaluation, moving from a positivist paradigm to an interpretive perspective; from a behaviorist theory of learning to a constructivist one; from emphasizing external incomes and factors to the concern for school procedures and pedagogical practices inside the classroom.

On the other hand, the need to improve the quality and validity of evaluation instruments has been revealed, leading to a tendency to focus evaluation on performance, standards, and classroom processes. Data analysis has extended to the use of multilevel hierarchical techniques.

National and international tests have been shown to be useful as evaluation data in order to provide a comparative perspective on the performance of educational systems. Nevertheless, this information does not yield solutions and forms of action at the intermediate level, such as provinces, municipalities, and schools where the action takes place. When referring to these levels, information about variables associated with the achievement of learning, and an appropriate model of analysis that reflects local reality and helps to define priorities and options to produce changes in pedagogic management of schools is needed.

This is why it is important to promote decentralized processes of evaluation that deal with the required diversity, the contexts, and factors related to success. This type of evaluation may serve as a complement for national examinations and give information that permits educational actors to take measures that improve education in their working teams. Longitudinal panel studies would be relevant here, following a sample of students over several years with the purpose of studying changes in their performance and the variables that influence it.

To face the problem of comparisons between students with different realities, it is important to work with added-value techniques. This has been a prominent development in England and France, for example, analyzing learning results in the context of the progress of each student and identifying associated variables (see Goldstein & Thomas, 1995). This information would be useful to recognize, within each school, its own diversity of learning paths and, at the same time, identify change strategies that vary from one institution to another or according to the profiles and characteristics of student cohorts.

Evaluation has not only undergone conceptual and methodological modification, but also a change of place within society. From a function exclusive to those who design policies and take decisions, it has shifted to a kind of evaluation that represents a tool for different actors in different moments in the process of shaping and implementing of policies.

This cyclical change in evaluation reflects a transformation in the relationship between states and societies, and in the distribution of knowledge about educational policies. Educational reforms do not continue to be thought of and executed exclusively by the state, and the concept of rationality that underlies the making of policies, experiences a profound change. There is a movement from technical rationality based on expert knowledge and the exclusive determination of decisions by administrative elites, to a form of rationality that rests on concepts of dialogue, argumentation, and conversation, stimulated by evaluation.

Today, the public agenda and the decisions taken are constructed throughout *conversational* spaces rather than inside a government board or at pinnacles of power. The public arena is not just the public authority's doings or governmental and state presence and action on society (Mény & Thoenig, 1989). On the contrary, 'the public' is to be understood as an encounter between state rationality and social will. It is government in and from a wide plural context. What we conceive as public is an intersection— a space that belongs to everyone (Laville, 2005; Patton, 1997; Pestoff, Osborne, & Brandsen, 2006; Vaillancourt, 2007). Inside this type of process, follow-up activities and evaluations are fundamental for the development of actors' discourses and the construction of the best solutions and policies for the problems that are to be encountered.

References

Baker, E., & Linn, R. (2002). *Validity issues for accountability systems.* Los Angeles, CA: Center for the Study of Evaluation. Retrieved from http://www.cse.ucla.edu/CRESST /Reports/TR585.pdf

Buendía Eximan, L., González González, D., Pozo Llorente, T., & Sánchez Núñez, C. A. (2004). Identidad y competencias interculturales. *RELIEVE, 10*(2), 135–183. Retrieved from http://www.uv.es/RELIEVE/v10n2/RELIEVEv10n2_1.htm

Candela, A. (1995) Transformaciones del conocimiento científico en el aula. In E. Rockwell (Ed.), *La escuela cotidiana* (pp. 173–197). México D.F., México: Fondo de Cultura Económica.

Carlson, B. (2000). ¿Qué nos enseñan las escuelas sobre la educación de los niños pobres de Chile? *Revista de la CEPAL, 72,* 165–184.

Coleman, J. (1966). *Equality of educational opportunity (the Coleman report).* Washington, DC: National Center for Educational Statistics.

Creemers, B. P. M. (1994). *The effective classroom.* London, England: Cassell.

Darling-Hammond, L. (2004). Standards, accountability, and school reform. *Teachers College Record, 106*(6), 1047–1085.

Edmonds, R. (1979). Effective school for the urban poor. *Educational Leadership, 37,* 15–27.

Ezpeleta, J., & Weiss, E. (2000). *Cambiar la escuela. Evaluación cualitativa del programa para abatir el rezago educativo.* México D.F., México: DIE.

Goldstein, H., & Thomas, S. (1995). School effectiveness and "value-added" analysis. *Forum, 37*(2), 36–38.

House, E. (1993). *Professional evaluation.* Thousand Oaks, CA: Sage.

Laville, J. L. (2005). *Sociologie des services. Entre marché et solidarité.* Paris, France: Eres.

Martinic, S. (2003). Representaciones de la desigualdad en la cultura escolar. In *Revista Persona y Sociedad, Ilades Working Papers, 17*(1), 129–146.

Mény, Y., & Thoenig, J. C. (1989). *Les politiques publiques.* Paris, France: PUF.

Muijs, D. (2003). La mejora y la eficacia de las escuelas en zonas desfavorecidas: Resumen de resultados de investigación. *Electronic Journal of Latin America on Quality, Effectiveness and Change in Education, 1*(2). Retrieved from www.ice.deusto.es /rinace/reice

Murillo, F. J. (Ed.). (2003). *La investigación sobre eficacia escolar en Iberoamérica. Revisión internacional del estado del arte.* Bogotá, Colombia: Convenio Andrés Bello.

Murillo, F. J. (2004). Mejora de la escuela: Para saber más. *Cuadernos de Pedagogía, 339,* 76–79.

Murillo, F. J. (2007). *Investigación Iberoamericana sobre eficacia escolar.* Bogotá, Colombia: Convenio Andrés Bello.

Murillo, J. (2005). La investigación en eficacia escolar y mejora de la escuela como motor para el incremento de la calidad educativa en Iberoamérica. *Revista Electrónica Iberoamericana sobre Calidad, Eficacia y Cambio en Educación, 3*(2). Retrieved from www.ice.deusto.es/rinace/reice

Norris, N. (1990). *Understanding educational evaluation.* London, England: Kogan Page.

OECD. (2003). *Knowledge research. New challenges for educational research.* Paris, France: OECD-CERI Publishing.

Ozlak, O. (1997). Estado y Sociedad. Colección CEA-CBC, *Las nuevas reglas de juego, 1.* Buenos Aires: UBA.

Ozlak, O. (1999, Octubre) Quemar las naves (o cómo lograr reformas estatales irreversibles). Ponencia presentada al *IV Congreso Internacional del CLAD.* México.

Patton, M. Q. (1997). Toward distinguishing empowerment evaluation and placing it in a larger context. *Evaluation Practice, 18*(2), 147–163.

Pestoff, V., Osborne, S. P., & Brandsen, T. (2006). Patterns of co-production in public services. Some concluding thoughts. *Public Management Review, 8*(4), 591–595.

Pini, E. M. (2000). Lineamientos de política educativa en los Estados Unidos: Debates actuales. Significados para America Latina. *Education Policy Analysis Archives, 8*(18). Retrieved from http://www.epaa.asu.edu/epaa/v8n18.html

Raczynski, D., & Muñoz, G. (2005). *Efectividad escolar y cambio educativo en condiciones de pobreza en Chile.* Santiago, Chile: Ministerio de Educación.

Ravela, P. (2001). *¿Cómo presentan sus resultados los sistemas nacionales de Evaluación Educativa en América Latina?* (PREAL Monograph). Santiago, Chile: PREAL.

Ravela, P., Picaroni, B., Fernández, T., Gonet, D., Haretche, C., Loureiro, G., & Luaces, O. (2000). *Evaluaciones nacionales de aprendizajes en Educación Primaria en el Uruguay (1995–1999).* Montevideo: Ed. UMRE-MECAEP-ANEP.

Ravela, P., Wolf, L., Valverde, R., & Esquivel, J. M. (2006). Los próximos pasos: ¿Cómo avanzar en la evaluación de aprendizajes en América Latina? (PREAL Monograph). Santiago, Chile: PREAL.

Ravitch, D. (1996, December). *Estándares nacionales en educación* (Working Papers). Santiago, Chile: PREAL.

Reynolds, D. (2010). *Failure-free education?: The past, present and future of school effectiveness and school improvement.* London, England: Routledge.

Rizvi, F. (2009). Globalisation and policy research in education. In K. Ryan & B. Cousins (Eds.), *The Sage international handbook of educational evaluation* (pp. 3–18). Thousand Oaks, CA: Sage.

Rockwell, E. (Ed.). (1995). *La escuela cotidiana.* México D.F., México: Fondo de Cultura Económica.

Sandoval, A., & Barrón, J. C. (2007). El programa de investigación del movimiento de escuelas eficaces: Hacia una perspectiva basada en los actores en el contexto de América Latina. *Revista electrónica Iberoamericana sobre calidad, eficacia y cambio en educación, 5*(5), 264–270. Retrieved from http://www.rinace.net/arts/vol5num5e/art36.pdf

Schiefelbein, E., & Farrel, J. (1975). La contribución de las diferencias en la calidad de la educación al nivel del rendimiento. En Schiefelbein y MacGinn, 35, Santiago, CPU.

Schwandt, T. (2009). Globalising influences on the Western evaluation imaginary. In K. Ryan & B. Cousins, *The Sage international handbook of educational evaluation* (pp. 19–36). Thousand Oaks, CA: Sage.

Shepard, L. (2000). The role of assessment in a learning culture. *Educational Researcher, 29*(7), 4–14.

Slavin, R. (1996). *Education for all.* Exton, PA: Swets & Zeitlinger Publishers.

Stake, R. E. (2004). *Standards based and responsive evaluation.* Thousand Oaks, CA: Sage.

Tylor, C., & Lyons, L. (1996). Theory-based evaluation. *Evaluation Practices, 17*(2), 177–184.

Vaillancourt, Y. (2007). *La co-construction des politiques publiques avec l'apport de l'économie sociale* (unpublished).

Wolf, L. (2006). *Las evaluaciones educacionales en América Latina. Avance actual y futuros desafíos* (PREAL Working Papers).

Zorrilla, M., & Ruíz, G. (2007). Validación de un modelo de mejora de la eficacia escolar en Iberoamérica. Factores de la escuela: Cultura para la mejora. El caso de México. *Revista Electrónica Iberoamericana sobre Calidad, Eficacia y Cambio en Educación, 5*(5), 200–204. Retrieved from http://www.rinace.net/arts/vol5num5e/art26.pdf

SERGIO MARTINIC *is professor of sociology at the Pontificia Universidad Católica de Chile, Faculty of Education.*

Guendel, L. (2012). Evaluation, public policies, and human rights. In S. Kushner &
E. Rotondo (Eds.), *Evaluation voices from Latin America. New Directions for Evaluation,*
134, 29–37.

3

Evaluation, Public Policies, and Human Rights

Ludwig Guendel

Abstract

The chapter addresses the role of social evaluation in the systematization of pub-
lic value and documents the adoption and implementation of public policy for
human rights. Public policy with a human rights approach arises from a polit-
ical, legal, and institutional acknowledgment of the social subject. It is an intri-
cate process, part of global discussions about how to reconfigure economic,
cultural, and social policy and the administration of justice. Its complexity
involves multiple dimensions and organizational and institutional processes as
they occur with any other government or state policy (Mény & Thoenig, 1992).
©Wiley Periodicals, Inc., and the American Evaluation Association.

Resumen

El capítulo aborda el papel de la evaluación social en la sistematización de valor
público, a fin de documentar la adopción y aplicación de políticas públicas para
los derechos humanos. Las políticas públicas con enfoque de derechos humanos
surgen de un reconocimiento político, jurídico e institucional del sujeto social.
Es un proceso complejo, que forma parte de las discusiones globales sobre cómo
volver a configurar la política económica, cultural y social y la administración
de justicia. Su complejidad involucra múltiples dimensiones y procesos organi-
zativos e institucionales que se producen con cualquier otro gobierno o la política
del estado (Mény & Thoenig, 1992). ©Wiley Periodicals, Inc., and the American Evaluation Association.

NEW DIRECTIONS FOR EVALUATION, no. 134, Summer 2012 © Wiley Periodicals, Inc., and the American Evaluation
Association. Published online in Wiley Online Library (wileyonlinelibrary.com) • DOI: 10.1002/ev.20016

The article reflects upon such complexities as public policy, human rights, and the evaluation process. I will argue that capturing institutional complexities through evaluation implies not only systematizing and understanding mainstreaming the human rights approach, but also conceptualizing human rights within a methodological strategy for evaluation. In any public policy, including its evaluation, there is a subjective dimension and a political dimension. "A representation of the social 'whole,' the State should also represent the world of the subjects. A State that does not contemplate the demands, motivations, feelings and affections of the people, renounces a crucial dimension to the social 'whole'" (Lechner, 1999).

Human Rights Approach

In recent years human rights approaches have been gaining strength, supported by international organizations like the United Nations, World Health Organization, and UNICEF. Human rights ceased being a matter of debate over the negative and exceptional aspects of who felt that their liberties were violated and turned into a positive dimension present in the social life of all the communities and individuals in a context of community integration and social cohesion. Likewise, human rights left the formalities of the courts and tribunals and transformed into specific demands on social movements of all types that aspired to the expansion and deepening of democracy and its liberties.

This new perspective on human rights and the philosophical debates around how universality is expressed in specificity, including acknowledgment of the subject, has been crystallized in the concept of the "human rights approach" (Jonsson, 2003). The human rights approach has also focused on an analysis of power in the context of legal norms and how these coincide with social norms. From this analysis specific and diverse aspects of rights emerge, such as universal equity; the eradication of child exploitation; the recognition of a complete sexuality for all people; the strengthening of social participation and social protection; recognition and respect for ethnic and cultural diversity; and global agreements on access to a basic level of welfare for all the people regardless of their sex, age, ethnicity, or social condition. The binomial social inclusion/exclusion, currently in fashion, expresses in positive and negative terms how human rights recognize or disclaim the different social groups and guarantee or limit the groups' liberty, autonomy, and access to future economic and social development.

The human rights approach is an institutional approach that bases access to rights on social agreements and on the existence of a framework of democratic governance. It is frequently assumed that this will lead to greater transparency, greater access to justice and services, greater equality and, consequently, superior levels of welfare.

The pressure of social movements and the adoption of this approach by the General Assembly of the United Nations, other international organizations, a wide range of conventions and declarations, and political regional conclaves such as the Pact of San José, create a significant breakthrough at the institutional level. Institutions are created specifically for this purpose (many Latin American governments have offices dedicated to the realization of the United Nations Millennium Development Goals, for example), and they stimulate development plans and agendas based on human rights, as well as debates about how this approach should be included among government policies at national and local levels. All types of programs and projects in the economic and social area are presumed to have adopted the human rights approach. It is a global movement.

At a regional level, agencies such as the Economic Commission for Latin America, Caribbean (ECLAC), international development agencies such as the United Nations Development Program, and financial organizations such as the World Bank and the Inter-American Development Bank see development from a more traditional point of view associated with governance, institutional capacities, and market value, but have more recently recognized the human rights–based approach. The incorporation of the human rights approach now constitutes a significant dimension to the efforts of all societies to secure economic, political, and social gains.

Paradoxically, along the way human rights ceased to be solely a matter of activists pushing for the specificity of rights. It is becoming the domain of lawyers and administrators of justice, tied more systematically into the moral and political fabric of public policy, the scope and limits of the market, and, in general, the values that govern our social practices (Cardenas, 2009). The shift is so noticeable that special advocates of children's rights, feminists, environmentalists, indigenous activists, and other proponents of human rights often express skepticism and at times complain that their demands and discourse are co-opted by government and are institutionalized. For some of these sectors, the movements in favor of human rights have lost their radical edge. Internal debates among these movements are intense; there are many conflicts of interest, as well as a great diversity of demands, positions, and points of view. Human rights transcend class-based argumentation and can barely be expressed on a single platform. They allude to cultural power relations that have an identity character that cuts across social structures.

Although the positioning of the rights-based approach develops in the institutional world, in the social sciences, and in the theory of development, it is also strengthened instrumentally in the operationalization of human rights. Lawyers approach social planners and advocate their thesis about the justice approach of rights (Abramovich, 2006), social programs are designed that adopt a human rights approach, social indicators are constructed for measuring compliance with rights agendas, and monitoring instruments are implemented for evaluations of policies and social programs.

Many of the technicians involved in the design of these new instruments may not have a deep understanding of the meaning of a human rights approach, but they contribute to the design of more precise instruments that identify the level of compliance with norms, access to information, levels of tax collection, and the other interests of rights administration. It is, therefore, necessary to be aware of the dangers of a technocratization of rights, which can lead to a new type of alienation. There is constant pressure to operationalize standards, establish control mechanisms, and prespecify results that in the end atomize the subject of rights. In fact, the neo-objectivization of rights (through administrative procedures) can once again leach social relations of their subjectivity, create a distance between owners and "managers" of rights, and build a rhetoric that reactivates a distance between the state and citizenship.

Assessment and Human Rights

Evaluation is a discipline that inquires into the process, performance, achievements, and impact of public policies and, more specifically, programs, projects, and activities (Subirats Humet, 2005). In Latin America evaluation is a recent discipline that has gained momentum in recent years. Several factors have contributed to this; among the most important are (a) concern about the scarcity of public resources, born of macroeconomic adjustments and the modernization and thinning of the State driven in the 1990s by neo-liberal efficiencies and neo-Keynesian efforts aimed at improving the capacity of the institutions; (b) a strengthening of the role of international cooperation and international financial agencies in the design and implementation of programs of social care, particularly those directed towards the alleviation of poverty; and (c) the professionalization of the social sciences and the development of the third sector, accompanied by a rationalization in the financial, technical, and administrative areas.

This period of social and economic adjustment was conducive to the development of diverse quantitative and qualitative methodologies, targeted at improving social learning. Many subsequent evaluation initiatives had a technocratic aspect and were framed as "monitoring and evaluation." The logic of projects helped the proliferation of all kinds of initiatives and produced a tendency to replace the political vision of public policy and assessments with a more sociological tint. Moreover, the eruption and growth of nongovernmental organizations (NGOs) coincided with the privatization, dispersion, and municipalization of social projects targeted at the poorest, which contributed to the search for a rapprochement with the beneficiaries of social programs and projects and to transforming the evaluation process into a more participatory process, though no less dispersed and fragmented.

Concerns regarding evaluation ceased to be a matter limited to international and government agencies and also involved social movements or citizens. These concerns about evaluation had already been stimulated by the emergence of NGOs, but these concerns now acquired greater strength and a more robust conceptual underpinning, especially because the idea of the subject reappeared from a perspective not dependent on the state for meaning, nor exclusively linked to productive spaces (such as subject as consumer). Also, the concern with evaluation involved another dimension never before seen in social management, namely, the relationship between the law and human rights. Indeed, following the adoption of Conventions and other international legal instruments that recognize specific rights such as for children, women, and indigenous groups, and that adapt national laws to these international standards, new methodologies emerged for monitoring and evaluating compliance with human rights. In traditional evaluation, the interest in impact is measured by access to resources and opportunities. Individual-based evaluation leads to questions about the theory of social change involved in public policies, programs, and projects, as well as its effects on institutions. Each individual is the person or social group that shares values, social regulations, and practices, formed through relations with others. A theory of change such as the human rights–based approach, whose purpose is to modify the value systems and regulations of organizations such as governments, private business, families, and society in general in order to introduce relationships with awareness of mutual acknowledgement, must, inevitably, affect basic concepts like maternity, paternity, sexuality, education, medicine, and the marketplace.

The human rights-based approach and social evaluation can be seen as intrinsically articulated concepts, because both rest upon judgment. The human rights–based approach is founded on the premise that the world has been organized around institutional strategies, leaving individuals behind. This approach aims to reestablish the importance of the individual. Social evaluation is, primarily, an evaluation act that wonders whether social public policies, programs, and projects are achieving results in terms of changing the living conditions of beneficiaries. From a human rights perspective, changes in livelihood conditions are not enough if they are not articulated with cultural and social changes aimed at transforming the basic terms of power relations. This leads to a consideration of how concepts like freedom, equal access, democratic participation, and acknowledgment are implemented through human rights. These must then become part of the agenda of evaluation.

At the outset such initiatives tended to be legalistic, though they eventually extended to a point where progress was made from rules and norms to public policy processes. Also, the citizens' movement shifted from a basis in demand to one of citizens' requirements and expectations, in fact, as a source of public education (Candau, 2001). This transition was accompanied by the development of a concept of more systematic evaluation and its production of knowledge and, indeed, with greater empirical grounding. This last contributed to the creation of instruments for measuring and systematizing real experience.

Understanding that a right is intrinsically articulated with public policy and that this is an expression and a guarantee of the recognition and the exercise of rights led to the analysis of public policy not only from its content but also from its fiscal underpinning and the ability to achieve concrete results in terms of gains in welfare and freedom. Rights and results were articulated as an expression of public accountability. In addition, the political dimension of public policy was explicitly recognized, which meant accepting the importance of advocacy to promote social mobilization that, in turn, strengthens the enforceability of rights.

Evaluation and its utilization by the citizen were vital instruments to achieve the given purposes. Evaluation became the catalyst for interesting initiatives such as high-profile reports on compliance with rights agreements and conventions. Social mechanisms emerged in Latin America such as 'Citizens Observatories' or independent bodies set up to scrutinize aspects of government policy and to inform the citizenry. (See, for example, the Ecuadorian Fiscal Policy Observatory: http://www.unicef.org/ecuador/policy_rights_3428.htm and the national project for social monitoring and public information in Costa Rica–State of the Nation: http://www.estadonacion .or.cr/.) These were frequently supported by United Nations agencies such as UNICEF, which adopted them as human rights initiatives. Social participation through such initiatives assumed a keener political sense. From the institutional perspective it abandoned the old thesis of a state of unrest of the social movements in competition with the state to collaborate with public policy. As a by-product, this also contributed to academic bodies and universities joining these processes, reconfiguring their links with society, this time from the perspective of citizens' advocacy, and increasingly through evaluative projects. Some examples in the field of childhood development and protection are the development of records of official achievement of rights that transform an evaluation act into a collective analysis with sometimes considerable impact on public accountability. There has been an emergence of organizations that systematically produce information and evaluation analysis to support arguments in favor of the enforceability of universal human rights.

In Mexico and other Latin American countries similar initiatives are developing. In the field of social investment there has been an effort to make budgets a matter of public information and transparency and to evaluate results. (See, for example, the Maringá Social Observatory in Brazil: http://www.cepal.org/dds/innovacionsocial/e/proyectos/br/maringa/.) This has generated strong social pressure to create deliberative communities and agencies formed by financial experts and professional politicians are expected to connect public expenditure with specific results in terms of human rights accomplishments. Ecuador, Paraguay, Costa Rica, Argentina, and Mexico have all mounted evaluations of this nature. These countries have incorporated human rights issues in public discourse, which, in turn, has contributed social change through institutional development.

NEW DIRECTIONS FOR EVALUATION • DOI: 10.1002/ev

The expansion of the public sphere caused by this deliberative concept of evaluation (see House & Howe, 1999) and the institutionalization of the recognition of rights has brought new problems of state management. It has implied the public engagement of actors explicitly oriented toward the evaluation of public policy in a constructivist sense and not in denial of governmental action, as happened in the past. This focus on human rights has created a citizens' demand for participation in state deliberations and the de facto recognition of citizen agencies that defend the rights of women, children, indigenous peoples, and Afro-descendants, which qualify themselves as representatives of citizenship. (Indeed, a major geopolitical shift in Latin America, partly accomplished through these means, has been the political accomplishments of indigenous groups in countries such as Ecuador and Paraguay.) Some of these agencies are supported and promoted by the state and have assumed the role of protection, demand, and denunciation, developing and institutionalizing evaluation acts of diverse nature.

There is no doubt that the rights discourse has generated new complexities and new challenges (Campbell, 2006; Villoria Mendieta, 2002). We realize the dangers of social fragmentation into multiple groups, which have a tendency to erode a global and articulated idea of social rights, remove them from the political arena, and present them only as specific or special rights. There is a risk of generating a new type of corporatism associated with organizations that express the identity-based interests of the new subjects of rights and causes tension to democracy. How do we reconcile two perspectives of recognition? The answer is specific rights with a vision of universal individual rights oriented to a deepening of democracy and a guarantee of rights for all (Uvin, 2004). This political challenge is a challenge for assessment and evaluation, which has to weave the particular into a vision of the holistic, overcoming the liberal idea of multiple groups competing in the context of a neutral and malleable state.

Rights in Public Policies and in Evaluation

To design, implement, and evaluate public policies with a human rights approach does not always serve to incorporate rights in public policies or in its assessment. The human rights approach lacks instrumentation and mechanisms that guarantee a discourse. For example, we evaluate rights-based programs, but there are few models of evaluation that are, themselves, rights based.

A human rights–based evaluation has to be centered in evaluating the conditions and the formative process of the social and political subject. Kushner (2002) postulates democratic evaluation, based on the evaluation of a program from the subject's point of view, what he calls "personalizing evaluation." His point of view is that the beneficiary of the policy, the program, or the project is conceived as a lens through which the program dynamic can be valued. Overall, the impact of social investment in a particular community is based on equity and social justice. This is not an anthropological perspective based on the testimony of the subjects, but rather on the reconstruction of a social world from the social programs that impact the quotidian world. Then the question arises as to whether an institutional and regulatory framework is designed or implemented to reflect the needs of the subject.

The following three dimensions of public policies and social evaluation involve different applications in terms of the intensity of the human rights–based approach and the aim to affect and put value into social issues from the individual point of view:

1. The economic dimension, which postulates the universal access to economic and social rights. This dimension leads to the analysis of the barriers to access and economic exclusion. There is a line of policy evaluation focused on factors that impede access to social policies and programs. Indeed, this is the more traditional and instrumental vision within the rights approach.

2. The cultural dimension, which is centered on what I distinguish as two perspectives. On the one hand, there are legal aspects, which suggest the incorporation of subjective rights into law and the administration of justice. This follows a recognition that the law has historically served the interest of particular groups in society and proposals for a positive law approach in response to universal human rights. In this sense, there is an effort required to evaluate positive law, the changes in legislation and its applications and scope in political and social life. On the other hand there are sociocultural aspects and proposals to modify the power of social relations through new social values based on a reconfiguration of social institutions. This dimension is usually ignored but it has great significance since it implies the incorporation of "right" in institutional procedures and in the analysis of intercultural relations. Also, from this perspective, the strengthening of political and social participation in the different spheres of the world is promoted, but from the point of view of identity as a constituent element of social power.

3. The political dimension associated with proposals for democratic governance based on the full exercise of citizenship, transparency, and other mechanisms of demand and democratic self-determination. This postulates the construction of a new consensus around the issue of human rights. Such initiatives lead to a public policy and its evaluation dedicated to the reform of political institutions that give a guarantee of training and development for active citizenship. From the evaluation perspective, this has involved a variety of new agencies and institutions, such as think tanks, and which develop new methodologies geared to enrich and expand the public sphere with new information and the analysis of social fragmentation.

Conclusions

Social evaluation is understood as a process that lifts the veil from public policy with the aim of improving its design, implementation, and impact. This acquires a particular nuance if it is seen from the approach of human rights. In the first place, the purpose of evaluation is not in itself confined to institutional or social structure, but rather to how the primacy of the subject is maintained. In the second place, because the evaluation of rights unravels political processes, power structures, and hegemonic relations to highlight the scope of the transformations that take place, it constitutes a political evaluation that points toward a strengthened democracy. This implies an obligation to present the point of view of the subject and to enrich the sphere of the public.

Methodologically the human rights approach requires a different concept of evaluation, one that is more personalized, more democratic, and with greater capacity to unveil intercultural and subjective aspects. In other words, the objective is to develop an evaluation that is centered on the subject. The debate centers on policies, the state, democracy, citizenship, and the intimacy of the person (Ryan & DeStefano, 2000). Social evaluation should question whether it is consistent with the purpose of achieving public policies when the subject is the primary focus, rather than structure.

References

Abramovich, V. (2006, abril). Una aproximación al enfoque de derechos en las estrategias y políticas de desarrollo. *Revista de la CEPAL, 88.*

Campbell, T. (2006). *Rights: A critical introduction.* London, England: Routledge.

Candau, V. M. (2001). *Human rights education in Latin America.* Munich, Germany: International Network Education for Democracy, Human Rights and Tolerance.

Cardenas, S. (2009). *Human rights in Latin America: A politics of terror and hope.* Philadelphia, PA: University of Pennsylvania Press.

House, E., & Howe, K. (1999). *Values in evaluation and social research.* Thousand Oaks, CA: Sage.

Jonsson, U. (2003). *Human rights approach to development programming.* Nairobi, Kenya: UNICEF.

Kushner, S. (2002). *Personalizar la evaluación.* Madrid, Spain: Ediciones Morata.

Lechner, N. (1999). El estado en el contexto de la modernidad. In N. Lechner, R. Millán, & U. Valdés (Eds.), *Francisco reforma del estado y coordinación social.* México D.F., México: Plaza y Valdez.

Mény, I., & Thoenig, J. C. (1992). *Las políticas públicas.* Barcelona, Spain: Ariel Ciencia Política.

Ryan, K., & De Stefano, L. (Eds.). (2000). *Evaluation as a democratic process: Inclusion, dialogue and deliberation. New Directions for Evaluation, 85.*

Subirats Humet, J. (2005). Catorce puntos esenciales sobre evaluación de políticas públicas con especial referencia al caso de las políticas sociales. *Economía, 60(1).*

Uvin, P. (2004). *Human rights and development.* Bloomfield, CT: Kumarian Press.

Villoria Mendieta, M. (2002, October). Control democrático y transparencia en la evaluación de políticas públicas. Paper presented at the 7th Congress of CLAD on the reform of the State and Public Administration, Lisbon, Portugal.

LUDWIG GUENDEL is a social theorist at the University of Costa Rica and served as deputy representative for UNICEF, Bolivia.

Faúndez Meléndez, A. (2012). Moving toward a gender equality and human rights perspective in evaluation. In S. Kushner & E. Rotondo (Eds.), *Evaluation voices from Latin
America. New Directions for Evaluation, 134*, 39–47.

4

Moving Toward a Gender Equality and Human Rights Perspective in Evaluation

Alejandra Faúndez Meléndez

Abstract

*This chapter concerns the emergence of a new perspective on evaluation based
on gender equality and human rights in Latin America and the Caribbean. As
in other regions of the world, there are many development challenges associated
with marginalized and excluded communities. In many Latin American countries, rights failures for indigenous cultures remain unresolved, and the way evaluation serves these peoples may not be immediately obvious, given cultural biases
in methodology. Some contributions of this focus on evaluation in general are
highlighted in this chapter, as well as both conceptual and methodological challenges faced, and future applications for this region. Finally, this article shares
some reflections that contribute to knowledge and debate on empowerment, identity development, and equity in Latin America and the Caribbean. ©Wiley Periodicals, Inc., and the American Evaluation Association.*

Resumen

*Este capítulo se refiere a la aparición de una nueva perspectiva en la evaluación
basada en la igualdad de género y los derechos humanos en América Latina y
el Caribe. Como en otras regiones del mundo, hay muchos retos de desarrollo
relacionados con las comunidades marginadas y excluidas. En muchos países de
América Latina se evidencian fracasos y los derechos de los pueblos indígenas
siguen sin resolverse, y la manera correcta en que la evaluación sirve a estos*

NEW DIRECTIONS FOR EVALUATION, no. 134, Summer 2012 © Wiley Periodicals, Inc., and the American Evaluation
Association.   Published online in Wiley Online Library (wileyonlinelibrary.com) • DOI: 10.1002/ev.20017

pueblos pueden no ser inmediatamente obvio, teniendo en cuenta los prejuicios culturales en la metodología. Algunas contribuciones de este enfoque para la evaluación en general se destacan en este capítulo, así como los desafíos conceptuales y metodológicos que enfrentan, y las aplicaciones de futuro para esta región. Finalmente, este artículo comparte algunas reflexiones que contribuyan al conocimiento y debate sobre el empoderamiento, el desarrollo con identidad, y la equidad en América Latina y el Caribe. ©Wiley Periodicals, Inc., and the American Evaluation Association.

This chapter focuses on the intersection of gender equity, human rights, and evaluation. To explore this intersection a number of sources have been used: First, it is the result of a systematic assessment carried out as a collaboration between the Office of Evaluation of UNWOMEN and the Inclusión y Equidad Consultancy. This assessment was conducted in 2010 and analyzed 21 evaluations from Latin America and the Caribbean carried out by UNIFEM, the Gender Equity Program of the Millennium Development Goal Achievement Fund (MDG-F), United Nations Development Program (UNDP), and the external evaluations from the Bolsa Familia programs from Brazil, Oportunidades from Mexico and Chile Solidario. At the same time, 12 support guides on the gender mainstreaming approach, which had been produced by NGOs, academic institutions, and government agencies, were reviewed. These guides were analyzed with specific reference to issues of tracking, monitoring, and evaluation. Second, this article includes an analysis of the opinions and contributions of a group of 61 experts in Latin America and the Caribbean, who met in Quito in February 2011 in a seminar entitled "Evaluation with a Gender and Human Rights Perspective: Measure or Transform Reality?" And finally, we include some reflections on our own evaluation practice (Abarca & Faúndez, 2012).

Importantly, the gender and human rights perspective in evaluation was implemented within the United Nations following a proposal of the United Nations Evaluation Group (UNEG), which, since 2010, has promoted the inclusion of elements of gender theory, consideration of stakeholders, cultural relevance in evaluation, and respect and promotion of human rights, throughout the evaluation processes and in its results (UNEG, 2011).

Equally, the production of training materials and instructions (manuals, support guides, online courses, etc.) on monitoring and evaluation that have been generated in the region in recent years is notable. This suggests that we are in a creative process of reflection and construction of a conceptual and methodological knowledge base.

The aim is to generate a new evaluation approach that is sensitive to gender equality and human rights. A review of those factors that facilitated this evaluation approach's origin and its current level of development in Latin America and the Caribbean suggests the following key elements (Abarca & Faúndez, 2012).

1. The progressive expansion of gender mainstreaming in the region (Pérez-Fragoso & Reyes, 2009) since 1995, with the Fourth World Conference on Women in Beijing. This has impacted various sectors and many organizations that design, implement, and evaluate public policies, generating methodologies and tools to consider and different outcomes for men and women.
2. A re-emergence of citizen participation, which has become increasingly institutionalized in the Latin American region. This can mean enhanced capacity for social movements to influence evaluation and citizen engagement in the shaping of public policy. This includes diverse experiences from the women's movement as well as other social movements. Environmentalists, indigenous peoples, and children, among others, have been promoting and setting up accountability and citizen control as part of their advocacy and training (Faúndez & Abarca, 2008).
3. The emergence of the human rights approach to the shaping of public policy. Starting in 1997, a set of reforms led by the Secretary General of the United Nations have led to the recovery of the notion of rights across the social policy spectrum. The UN Common Understanding on a Human Rights-Based Approach in 2003, the UN's Declaration on the Rights of Indigenous Peoples in 2007, and earlier declarations for women and children, along with the enactment of explicit guarantees for the exercise of rights by some governments in the region, have created conditions for operationalizing human rights in the form of dedicated development programs (Sanz Luque, 2010).
4. A public discourse around evaluation itself. International conferences, the emergence of numerous evaluation networks and societies, as well as new documentation and training processes have promoted the case for ethical, operational, and regulatory frameworks that allow creation of a specifically Latin American knowledge-base on evaluation issues (Sanz Luque, 2010).
5. The conceptual and operational framework of results-based management (RBM) and development effectiveness. This translates into an effort to measure better the results of policies, plans, programs, and projects in different areas as a base for public accountability. Progressively, it has come to be understood that "development is something that happens to people" (Segone, 1998) and thus, all results (positive, negative, intended, and unintended) of a development intervention, are about diverse people and their communities. This experience has also repositioned the importance of evaluation in the project cycle and raises the need to improve information and indicators about outcomes for women and men (DAC, 2008).
6. Moreover, we are witnessing a growing process of institutionalization in this field. In past decades, evaluation mechanisms were created within large multinational organizations like the World Bank and the

Inter-American Development Bank, both in the United Nations system. Additionally, the establishment of the International Organization for Co-operation on Evaluation (IOCE), ReLAC (Evaluation Network for Latin America), Network for Monitoring and Evaluation in Latin America and the Caribbean (REDLACME) have emerged in recent years, along with the creation of specialized institutions in the public sector. There are already several countries that have built specific evaluation agencies and thus are expanding the policy framework of public institutions in this field.

Finally, it is important to consider that Latin America and the Caribbean have their own distinguishing features: the presence of indigenous peoples, Afro-descendant populations, and the unique fabric of civil society. This poses challenges for evaluation, in terms of documenting exclusion, historical discrimination against certain groups including the denial of language, and the geopolitical shifts taking place as indigenous peoples are successfully politicized (as in Bolivia and Ecuador).

Thus, in recent years these elements have begun to come together, with different nuances, to create a progressive and constructive evaluation process with a gender equality and human rights orientation. We are in a situation that is complex, but provides space for dialogue between different views, knowledge, and perspectives on the role, shaping, and strategies of evaluation. At the same time, of course, there is a predominant view of evaluation as a culturally neutral technology that can generate quality-of-life indicators that are universal and comparable, including much of the work measuring progress toward Millennium Development Goal accomplishment.

Implications for the Integration of a Gender and Human Rights Perspective in the Region From a Conceptual Point of View

A transformation of the concept of gender (commonly used as a synonym for women) to a more complex concept than biological sex: "it analyzes the historical synthesis of the relationship between the biological, economic, social, legal, political, psychological and cultural aspects; sex is implied, but analysis does not stop there" (Lagarde, 1996). This demands that evaluation involve analytical capacities for gender appraisal: considering the relational aspects between men and women, analyzing differential access and control of resources, personal time use, participation in decision-making, and intersections with other dimensions such as race and ethnicity. It also implies expanding the concept of "women." Women often are visible to development agencies and evaluation sponsors only in their role as mothers or in their condition of "poverty and vulnerability." Both conceptualizations are reductionist, limiting the role of women in development, and have been criticized, starting in the early 1990s when Gender and Development (GAD) emerged, replacing the older paradigm of Women in Development (WID) (Moser, 1993).

At the same time some foundational meanings and concepts in evaluation are being questioned. Studies on health care quality for rural women, for example, have brought to light the need for revising concepts such as effectiveness. These should be based on the meanings and judgments that users and beneficiaries of public services give to those concepts, which can be notably different from the meanings that rural health care providers, for example, give them (Anderson, 2001) or, indeed, different from those of international aid agencies. There is a role for evaluation to sensitize development agencies and governments to cultural and gender differences.

With respect to human rights, there is a similar phenomenon. The human rights perspective gives us an ethical and normative consensus, and a valid framework for all countries, which has the force of legitimacy given to it by the international community. Nevertheless, it is important that the field of evaluation develop concepts of human development and human rights, expanding freedoms and capacities to go above and beyond the economic dimension found in traditional theories of development (Sen, 1990).

Moreover, from a gender perspective, internationally recognized human rights will inevitably begin to be more inclusive of the female experience. The fact that women were incorporated into these discussions on human rights and development and that the UN has a dedicated agency for promoting women's rights has had an impact on dominant approaches (Anderson, 1992; Guzmán, Portocarrero, & Vargas, 1991; Kabeer, 2006; Lagarde, 1994; Moser, 1995). For example, evaluations of economic projects frequently make women invisible and undervalue women's productive and reproductive work, because of the use of traditional definitions of work (Espino, 2009). Some evaluations of the contribution of women's work to a national economy have shown that women's unpaid reproductive work makes significant contributions to the gross national product (GNP): "The economists that have tried to measure the importance of the non-market sector in relation to total economic activity, conclude that in the most advanced economies, this sector contributes significantly to total production" (Carrasco, 1991). These kinds of measurements will have an important impact on the way work is conceptualized, and will show the limitations of national accounts, the relationships between monetary and nonmonetary economies, and, at the same time, how to measure these phenomena.

Exercise, Promotion, and Protection of Rights

A stronger connection has been developed between the Universal Declaration of Human Rights and the realization and concrete evaluation of those rights. The existence of international instruments such as the Convention on the Elimination of all Forms of Discrimination against Women (CEDAW) and the Inter-American Convention to Prevent, Sanction, and Eradicate Violence Against Women (Convention of Belém Do Pará), which are binding for ratifying countries, offer a standard for the changes that are hoped to be achieved, in the language of human rights.

With respect to indigenous peoples the existence of Convention 169 of the International Labor Organization (ILO), as well as the UN Declaration on the Rights of Indigenous Peoples, raises questions about the cultural orientation of methodologies that are typically used to evaluate those projects that directly affect indigenous peoples. Currently, some governments in the region and some multilateral organizations are using consultation mechanisms and safeguards that guarantee the exercise of rights, and look for mitigation strategies when there is a risk that those rights may be violated. This prevents the evaluation process from reinforcing patterns of gender exclusion and reducing or limiting the exercise of human rights, as has historically occurred. These elements have had a concrete impact on monitoring systems, indicators, classic information-gathering methods, and other evaluation instruments. Even so, there has still not emerged a rights-based approach to evaluation itself—other than conventional participatory methods.

Conclusions

The visibility of gender inequity has been dependent on disaggregated data by sex, age, ethnicity and race, etc., provided by official statistics (censuses, surveys, and administrative records). Only in the past few decades has such information begun to become available, and in several countries in the region, that data are still precarious and discontinuous. There are data management systems with specific focus on the Latin American region, such as DevInfo (LAC) and the Multiple Indicators Cluster (Household) Survey, and ECLAC is charged with generating data sets of development issues. Even here, however, data quality is highly variable, and there are significant problems in data harmonization, leading to occasional confusion and disagreement on, for example, the accomplishment of Millennium Development Goals. Even then, data sets still do not reflect the particularities of indigenous experience and quality of life. The representation of issues to do with gender and cultural inequities remains a major challenge.

This also requires us to consider the disposition behind changes that are happening in different areas of development: Evaluation should address the values base of social policy and interventions. This demands the emergence of more searching evaluation methods, including those designed to reveal the workings of power systems and that challenge the evaluator to move beyond a conventional narrow focus. "Rigid approaches to reporting on targets/indicators/outputs/outcomes that were planned at the start of a change intervention are not useful in women's rights and empowerment work" (Batliwala, 2011).

Missing from the evaluations that were reviewed is the dimension of power. It would appear that the relationships between civil society organizations and governments were assumed to flow without conflict or disturbance, as if competing interests did not exist. However, transactions and conflicts of interest that exist at the boundaries of different social constituencies should be more visible in evaluation. The tensions that result from exercising power in evaluative processes should be made explicit.

An agenda for addressing such issues would start with

1. A specific focus on how interventions have positively or negatively affected gender equality and women's empowerment, as well as any other group that faces discrimination when exercising their rights. This should cast evaluation in terms of House's (1980) principle of evaluation promoting fairness and social justice and discriminating in favors of the least advantaged.
2. Review and reform the evaluative process from design, selection of methods and techniques, data collection, and analysis, to applying results. This implies a change in focus in what to evaluate and how to evaluate it.
3. Extensively involve all interested parties, promoting their empowerment through participation and inclusion so as to bring evaluation into the arena of citizen rights. Following House (1980), special emphasis should be placed on the most discriminated groups, whose voices have historically been left out of evaluative processes.
4. Adapt appropriate evaluative tools to the cultural particularities of each group or community, to take into account their interests, needs, quality-of-life perceptions, and values. For this, capacity building and strengthening of civil society institutions that are allied to evaluation development is important.
5. Consider the cultural and gender dimensions of evaluation ethics.
6. Better and more systematic links to international human rights instruments (especially those which are mandatory) and the results of assessments in the region. Progress is possible in the exercise of human rights and gender equality through policy instruments and the assessment itself.

References

Abarca, H., & Faúndez, A. (2012). *Enfoque de igualdad de género y derechos humanos en la evaluación. Sistematización de la práctica en América Latina y el Caribe*. Nueva York, NY: ONU Mujeres y Consultora Inclusión y Equidad (en prensa).

Anderson, J. (1992). *Intereses o justicia: ¿A dónde va la discusión sobre la mujer y el desarrollo?* Cuadernos de Trabajo, Red Entre Mujeres: Un Diálogo Sur-Norte. Lima, Perú.

Anderson, J. (2001). *Tendiendo puentes. Calidad de atención desde la perspectiva de las mujeres rurales y de los proveedores de servicios de salud*. Lima, Perú: Movimiento Manuela Ramos.

Batliwala, S. (2011). *Strengthening monitoring and evaluation for women's rights: Thirteen insights for women's organizations.* Toronto, Canada: Association for Women's Rights in Development (AWID).

Batliwala, S., & Pittman, A. (2010). *Capturing change in women's realities: A critical overview of current monitoring, evaluation frameworks and approaches.* Toronto, Canada: The Association for Women's Rights in Development (AWID). Retrieved from http://www.awid.org/About-AWID/AWID-News/Capturing-Change-in-Women-s-Realities

Carrasco, C. (1991). *El trabajo doméstico. Un análisis económico.* Madrid, Spain: Ministerio de Trabajo y Seguridad Social de España.

Development Assistance Committee (DAC). (2008). *Guiding principles of CAD on aid effectiveness, gender equality and empowerment of women.* Paris, France: OECD.

Espino, A. (2009). *América Latina: Equidad de género, comercio internacional y desarrollo. Manual de capacitación.* Buenos Aires, Argentina: Red Internacional de Género y Comercio, Ministerio de la Igualdad de España, Federación de Mujeres Progresistas, IGTN.

Faúndez, A. (2007). *¿Qué entendemos por enfoques de género?* Serie Marcos conceptuales. Santiago de Chile: Consultora Inclusión y Equidad.

Faúndez, A. (2010). *La evaluación con enfoque de género, lecciones desde la experiencia.* Paper presented at the Conference of the Network Monitoring, Evaluation and Systematization of Latin America and the Caribbean (ReLAC), San José, Costa Rica.

Faúndez, A., & Abarca, H. (2008). *Más participación, más democracia. Mecanismos de participación de la sociedad civil en Iberoamérica.* In IV Ibero-American Civic Meeting in the context of the Thirteenth Ibero-American Summit of Presidents and Heads of State. San Salvador, El Salvador: SEGIB.

Guzmán, V., Portocarrero, P., & Vargas, V. (1991). *Una nueva lectura: Género en el desarrollo.* Lima, Perú: Flora Tristán Ediciones.

House, E. (1980). *Evaluating with validity.* Thousand Oaks, CA: Sage.

Kabeer, N. (2006). *Lugar preponderante del género en la erradicación de la pobreza y las metas de desarrollo del milenio* (1st ed.). México D.F., México: Centro Internacional de Investigaciones para el Desarrollo, Plaza y Valdés Editores.

Lagarde, M. (1994). La regulación social del género: El género como filtro de poder. In *Enciclopedia de la sexualidad* (pp. 389–425). México D.F., México: Consejo Nacional de Población.

Lagarde, M. (1996). La multidimensionalidad de la categoría de género y del feminismo. In M. L. González Marín (Coord.), *Metodología para los estudios de género.* México D.F., México: Instituto de Investigaciones Económicas, Universidad Nacional Autónoma de México.

Moser, C. (1993). *Gender, planning and development.* London, England: Routledge.

Moser, C. (1995). *Planificación de género y desarrollo. Teoría, práctica y capacitación.* Lima, Perú: Red Entre Mujeres. Flora Tristán Ediciones.

Pérez-Fragoso, L., & Reyes, E. (2009). *Transversalización de la perspectiva de equidad de género. Propuesta metodológica y experiencias. Equidad de género: Ciudadanía trabajo y familia.* México D.F., México: A.C. y Unión Europea.

Sanz Luque, B. (2010). Gender equality and human rights responsive evaluation: Rethinking approaches. In M. Segone (Ed.), *From policies to results. Developing capacities for country monitoring and evaluation systems.* France: UNICEF, DevInfo, IDEAS, ILO, IOCE, The World Bank, UNDP, UNIFEM, WFP.

Segone, M. (1998). *Democratic evaluation* (Working Paper No. 3). Regional Office for Latin America and the Caribbean, UNICEF.

Sen, A. (1990). Development as capability expansion. In K. Griffin & J. Knight (Eds.), *Human development and the international development strategy for the 1990s.* London, England: MacMillan.

UNEG. (2010). *Handbook for integrating human rights and gender equality perspectives in evaluations in the UN system.* New York, NY: United Nations.

UNEG. (2011). *Integrating human rights and gender equality in evaluation.* New York, NY: United Nations.

ALEJANDRA FAÚNDEZ MELÉNDEZ is a lecturer and researcher in evaluation, gender perspectives, social indicators, and inclusive public policies, and is currently a member of the CREFAL; ReLAC; Regional Centre for Latin America and the Caribbean of UNDP, and is the Latin American director of Inclusión y Equidad Consultancy.

NEW DIRECTIONS FOR EVALUATION • DOI: 10.1002/ev

5

Youth Participation in Evaluation: The Pró-Menino Program in Brazil

*Daniel Braga Brandão, Rogério Renato Silva,
Renata Codas*

Abstract

*This chapter reports a participatory evaluation conducted in Brazil, where
youngsters with life pathways marked by involvement in crime, and therefore
included in social programs, were invited to be the evaluation team of the program. The experience provokes reflections on new technical and ethical challenges in the evaluation process. The authors also present a new methodological
proposal for the field of qualitative investigations created exclusively for this
evaluation, called FRAMES (QUADROS), which is inspired by comic books. The
broad ethical frame is a positive "capabilities" approach to evaluative work with
youth.* ©Wiley Periodicals, Inc., and the American Evaluation Association.

Resumen

*Este artículo presenta una evaluación participativa realizada en Brasil, donde
los jóvenes con las vías de la vida marcadas por la participación en el crimen, y
por lo tanto incluidos en los programas sociales, fueron invitados a actuar como
parte del equipo de evaluación del propio programa. La experiencia provoca la
reflexión sobre los nuevos desafíos técnicos y éticos en el proceso de evaluación.
El texto también presenta, en pocas palabras, una nueva propuesta metodológica para el campo de la investigación cualitativa creado exclusivamente para
esta evaluación, llamados MARCOS (QUADROS) e inspirado por los cómics.*

NEW DIRECTIONS FOR EVALUATION, no. 134, Summer 2012 © Wiley Periodicals, Inc., and the American Evaluation
Association. Published online in Wiley Online Library (wileyonlinelibrary.com) • DOI: 10.1002/ev.20018

El marco ético amplio es el enfoque positivo "capacidades" para trabajar con los jóvenes de evaluación. ©Wiley Periodicals, Inc., and the American Evaluation Association.

U rban violence is among the most serious of social problems in Brazil, and its main victims are youngsters, especially African-Brazilians and those living in urban outskirts (Waiselfisz, 2004). Their involvement in crime is one of the more worrisome aspects of this phenomenon as it is often life-threatening and requires significant investment to bring about change.

Brazilian legislation includes an advanced legal instrument, the Statute on Children and Adolescents (ECA), which governs the rights of the under-18-year-old population and stipulates legal procedures to be fulfilled by young offenders. These procedures are called social-educative procedures (MSE-MA) and can be fulfilled under restricted movement (confinement) or unrestricted movement (in liberty). Primarily, the ECA statute recommends an offending adolescent fulfill a social-educative procedure within the community designed to preserve their freedom and establish a commitment to disciplined participation in educational opportunities offered by the state or by civil society organizations (CSOs).

MSE-MAs are funded by the government and are not readily sponsored by the private sector. An exception is the Pró-Menino Program developed by Telefonica Foundation in the state of São Paulo, which is an important initiative partnering governmental and nongovernmental organizations to assist adolescents in fulfilling an MSE-MA.

The Pró-Menino Program is aimed at breaking the adolescent-crime link, through 1- or 2-year investments in organizations that carry out MSE-MAs and that are committed to the improvement or their technical staff, as well as developing information technology activities with youngsters, thus helping to overcome digital exclusion and offering them new forms of social communication and relationships (recent world events have shown how important this is to youth agency and inclusion in social and political life).

After six consecutive years of investment in a considerable number of municipalities in the State of São Paulo, Telefonica Foundation saw the need for an external evaluation of the program. They sought to build learning capabilities within the program, influence future investments, and contribute to public debate on the relations between youth, crime, and the MSE-MA strategies.

A Participatory Evaluation Approach

The Fonte Institute for Social Development was invited to conduct the evaluation of the Pró-Menino Program in Brazil. The Fonte Institute is recognized for implementing participatory processes directed at formative evaluative learning of stakeholders (Brandão, 2007; Dussel, 2002; Freire, 1996; Guba & Lincoln, 1989; House & Howe, 1999; Kaplan, 2005).

In considering the totality of projects supported by the program and according to Telefonica Foundation guidance, four organizations (three NGOs and one organization associated with the local municipal government) who provided assistance to adolescents fulfilling MSE-MAs were included in the evaluation planning. Each organization had been supported since 2005 and was located in different municipalities in the state of São Paulo. From the very beginning, identification of the evaluation questions, with criteria and indicators, was based on the needs and desires of each one of these social actors. From this dialogue, the focus of the evaluation was established as the then-current (in 2007) social and economic situation of the adolescents and youngsters who had fulfilled MSE-MAs in 2005, that is, 2 years after the project. With that aim, a sample of 1,398 adolescents scattered in the outlying districts of four municipalities were identified as a population that would be reached by the evaluation to gather information on seven dimensions: family status, school, work, health, housing, violence, and digital inclusion.

The Ethical Challenge

Within the evaluation we faced the challenge of incorporating the youth into the evaluation process. According to Dussel (2002), the universal material criterion of ethics is human life; any aspect that touches its development defines an ethical field. In order to address these issues in the Pró-Menino evaluation, youngsters fulfilling MSE-MAs were included in the decision making about the evaluation, thereby allowing them to influence a program that directly affected their lives. These youngsters, marked by social exclusion and stigmatized for their involvement in crime, created the possibility for the evaluation to serve as a forum for debate and the potential for learning among the stakeholders, and hopefully lead to decisions not associated with traditional institutional and hierarchical structure.

There was, however, a technical issue associated with the ethical challenge that had profound consequences for the quality of the work. The evaluation required offending adolescents and interviewers to meet, the former identified by their previous involvement in crime, the latter identified by the need to interview youngsters about a range of potentially charged and intimate matters. We anticipated that an interviewer detached from the adolescent's universe might reinforce the likelihood of inauthentic answers from youth in order not to expose him or herself to delicate situations, such as revealing that the youth had committed a new offense after fulfilling the MSE-MA.

One way to deal with this technical–ethical challenge was to establish a team of interviewers composed of youngsters who were fulfilling or who had fulfilled MSE-MAs in the same organizations participating in the evaluation. Within that scope, young evaluators would form a group capable of discussing and interacting (ethically) within the evaluation process, thus constituting a group of stakeholder–peers. The interviewer–interviewee meeting therefore generated the possibility of building a quasihorizontal relationship within the cultural universes of both interviewer and interviewee, offering a higher degree of symmetry. Marked by shared language and stories potentially developed through complicity, the dialogue presented in the interview allowed the sharing of memories, information, and feelings, with an authenticity that might be difficult to achieve otherwise.

Youngsters With a Key Role in the Evaluation

The leading role of youngsters participating in the evaluation of social projects is a subject recently discussed in evaluation practice and literature (Gong & Wright, 2007; Walker, 2007; Whitmore & McKee, 2001). Walker (2007) summarizes Horsch et al. (2002) five key elements for the involvement of youngsters in research projects: (a) organizational and community readiness, (b) adequate training and support for involved youth, (c) adequate training and support for adult staff, (d) selecting the right team, and (e) sustaining youth involvement.

Within the context of evaluation of the Pró-Menino Program, it was essential to establish a rigorous selection process for young evaluators, as team quality would support the study's internal validity. The selection process of young evaluators consisted of four stages: (a) nominations by the educators of partner organizations, according to profiles suggested by the Fonte Institute; (b) submission of résumés by the appointed youngsters; (c) individual interviews with the candidates; and (d) administration of human resource selection tests (under the guidance of a specialized company).

It is worth noting that the entire selection cycle assumed a strong pedagogical intent, as it characterized a milestone in the lives of the youngsters entering the employment market. Twenty-nine interviews were conducted to select eight adolescents. The selection team's challenge was to be guided by previously agreed-upon criteria. The particular life circumstances of the youngsters undeniably presented a possibility for their exclusion and to deny them a new way to relate to the world. In two cases this occurred, but the adolescents were hired. By the end of the evaluation, the selection of one proved to be successful, whereas the other youngster came to be the source of some conflict with partners. Local monitors were selected in parallel with the hiring of the youngsters. Monitors were also young residents in one of the four cities where the evaluation was conducted and were responsible for follow-up of the work routine of the young evaluators. The monitors had two assignments: quality control of the work (time, behavior, task completion) and education (problematize, facilitate reflection, and identify learning from past experiences). Monitors were essential for the proper conduct of the evaluation as they allowed daily, systematic, and disciplined follow-up of the adolescents, a characteristic which is relatively rare in their lives. At the center of the evaluation there was a coordinating team comprising two authors of this article. The eight adolescents eventually selected for the job were hired with due regard to the conditions provided in the Brazilian Labor legislation, with a net salary of approximately US$240.00 per month and a weekly workload of 30 hours. They were also granted support for transportation and meals.

In order to undertake their roles in this evaluation, the youngsters needed to develop specific competences. Preparation took place initially at a seminar, where the adolescent's assignments were discussed and doing interviews was practiced. The interview questions were finalized during this process. Previously prepared questions were discussed by the adolescents, and as a consequence there were adaptations in the language used to make the interview appropriate for the prospective interviewees. A pilot test was conducted with youngsters from a nearby community and from then onwards the field stage was initiated.

Although marked by euphoria and enthusiasm for the new work, the seminar also presented a number of delicate situations. There was drug abuse, and conflict arose among the girls. These were taken as an educational opportunity for an in-depth discussion in which the actions were made explicit and discussed. The effect of this discussion was crucial in changing the attitude of the adolescents in relation to the work and formed the basis for new dialogues that were held during the following months. The premise in the relationship with the adolescents was to use every event as a learning opportunity. Nothing was to be ignored and, evidently, the evaluation team itself was also to face new and unusual situations.

Continuity of group education took place on a day-to-day basis, informally, with support from the monitors and from the evaluation team. Two formal meetings were held. One was conducted halfway through the process to analyze the ongoing process of the survey and to reflect on strategies, and the other was held at the end of the process to formalize the conclusion of the work.

Young Evaluators' Role

Gaining access to young interviewees in the target population was a challenge. The quality of contact lists provided by organizations, for example, was poor. In order to make invitations for interviews, telephone calls were prioritized and, in some cases, it was necessary to send telegrams and letters. The youngsters made the calls, trying to convince former participants of the program to participate in interviews. This was the first moment in which common and appropriate language was used between adolescent interviewers and interviewees. This stage aimed to gather primary data on the status of the population in the evaluation. Thirty-five percent of the population we contacted, representing 133 youngsters, were unable to participate in the evaluation because they were in jail ($n = 103$; 78%), had died ($n = 18$; 13.5%), or were missing or had been threatened with death ($n = 12$; 8.3%). Such data clearly showed evidence of the level of violence experienced by this population. Nevertheless, the structural outline of this work limited the evaluation to youngsters at liberty, and it was not possible to interview those imprisoned. In the first stage, questionnaires were administered at the organizations where the youngster had fulfilled his or her MSE-MA. Concentrating the execution of this task at a single place helped guarantee greater follow-up of the young evaluators' actions. Youngsters were encouraged to participate in the evaluation by receiving pay for their transportation to the organization and also by receiving a small gift. The implementation of the evaluation on a day-to-day basis was managed by coordinators working at maintaining constant communication with the municipalities where the interviews were being conducted. A blog with limited access was created so that work experiences could be shared and also with the aim of encouraging young evaluators to write. Some visits were made with the purpose of motivating local teams and of resolving occasional conflicts between young evaluators and monitors. These conflicts were always solved through dialogue (individual and in groups) with all the parties involved in the situation. At the end of this first stage, a work-monitoring meeting was held to enable the entire team to consider results, describe learning experiences, and contribute to the strategic continuity of the questionnaires.

The second stage of questionnaire administration was marked by seeking out youngsters where they lived. Such incursions into the communities increased risks for the team; however, it was essential to augment the 176 questionnaires from the previous stage and, simultaneously, to add to the sample youngsters who had not been willing or able to go to the organization where they had fulfilled an MSE-MA. The assumption was that the first set of youngsters represented a subpopulation that was more connected to the organizations and for that reason more likely to positively influence survey results. On the other hand, youngsters who established fragile connections, who were still linked to crime, or who experienced greater social exclusion, might be more likely to decline the initial invitation. During the second stage, 73 (29% of the total) questionnaires were applied in different environments: residences, bars, on the streets, and even at drug-trafficking points.

Once all the data were collected, the young evaluators dedicated themselves to preparing the interview results for statistical analysis. This period of analysis was particularly challenging, because it characterized a moment when others were conducting the statistical analysis, which resulted in a period of inactivity for the youngsters. In an attempt to deal with idleness the youth were asked to elaborate upon reports (yet another effort to stimulate the practice of writing), and study the ECA statute or other subjects that would subsequently provide them with evidence to discuss the results. However, these suggestions had little take-up among the youngsters. There was an attempt to discuss alternatives, but, nothing productive was achieved, in contrast with the dynamic fieldwork of applying questionnaires, which the youth found quite stimulating. Once the data were analyzed, they were sent to the teams of each municipality so that each one could prepare presentations for the groups of educators from the MSE-MA assistance organizations. This activity required the development of some computer skills, as well as an understanding of the information obtained. One-day presentation dates were scheduled at each municipality; these events were taken seriously by many of the youth. We observed some of the youngsters in formal attire, proudly presenting evaluation results to those who had been their educators. Youngsters had absolute autonomy regarding the presentations. They were free to present the results in their own way and in their own style: one group made a video presentation and the others used PowerPoint. Evaluation coordinators were expected to contribute with one another with comments or questions that might stimulate the debate. This was the space in which equal participation in the evaluations was achieved, beyond the evaluation team's data-collection activities. Symmetrical discursive communities (Dussel, 2002) were created that enabled horizontal discussions within an environment where the previously excluded had the power to speak up. The meeting between youngsters and the Executive Board of Telefonica Foundation was yet another moment with similar resonance. To conclude this stage of the evaluation, a seminar was proposed with the purpose of critically discussing the evaluation experience with the youngsters in order to reinforce acquired knowledge, as well as preparing them for the conclusion of the work and better preparing them to face the employment market. Surprisingly, the meeting was of little interest to the adolescents. Concern with the conclusion of the work and with placement in another income-generating activity seemed to be of much more concern to the coordinating team than to the adolescents themselves. The need to perform well in order to qualify for the evaluation work, which was a strong point in the first meeting, no longer prevailed.

Knowledge Gained From Working With Young Evaluators

The experience of working with the evaluation meant a great deal to the youngsters involved and provided the opportunity to face a new challenge with proper working conditions, within an institutional structure. At first, the young evaluators seemed motivated by the work and wages. On the other hand, the Fonte Institute team hoped the youth would participate in debates and reflections, and expected them to learn. These different motivations required constant realignment of expectations in a systematic search for the understanding of both (coordinators and young evaluators), so work results would adequately satisfy all those interested.

In that sense, the creation of a critical orientation to debate was a serious challenge for the coordinating team, which was only partially satisfied at the conclusion of the project. Deep down, expectations regarding this level of participation were too high for the circumstances and for the profile of the work team. Nonetheless, the impact that an initiative of this nature had on the lives of these youngsters is noteworthy. Self-esteem was raised, life projects were conceived, relationships with educators from partner organizations matured, and even improvements in family relationships were observed. The horizontal characteristic of the conversation created by the young evaluators in meeting with the interviewees seemed also to have brought the desired effects. Good evidence of this is the presence of sensitive data at consistent and even concerning levels, such as the index of youngsters who admitted to having committed new offenses after having fulfilled a MSE-MA ($n = 70$; 28.1%).

One aspect of this work discussed by Walker (2007) is the involvement of educators from participating organizations in the evaluation. We acknowledge there was good communication throughout the evaluation, which, however, could have reached further depth at several time points, such as providing a more consistent debate during the selection process, which could better guide the decisions of the coordinating team.

Reflecting on the selection process, it seems clear now that acting solely on objective criteria is complicated in the life scenario of these youngsters and, particularly, in the relationship established among them and those who select them. Adopting the youngster's exclusion status as a hiring criterion was of relevance for this evaluation, which meant acknowledging the evaluation process as an intervention in the pathway of these individuals lives. There is no doubt that, recognizing the need for such an intervention, the evaluation process must also have pedagogical rigor, increasing the challenge of the work. The formality of the employment agreement, which demanded from the young evaluators a certain number of hours of weekly engagement, resulted in situations in which performativity was limited and where team morale tended to diminish. Fluctuations in the intensity of the evaluation workload were reflected in the mood changes of the group. It was a challenge to sustain a repertoire of strategies to maintain young evaluators constantly involved in evaluation-related actions. Finally, it is clear that the participatory strategy made the operation of the evaluation more complex and required constant strategic reflection.

The results obtained through this process impacted the organizations involved in the program differently. The evaluation was important for the funding foundation. It showed the relevance of having adopted an active role in politics in incorporating into its project-financing work the responsibility for creating public spaces for debate, adopting a critical stance regarding the topic, and connecting with relevant political actors.

Both this bold proposal and the data collected encouraged the Foundation to publish a book (see http://institutofonte.org.br/vozes-e-olhares) that describes the evaluation process and presents the results found. The book launch itself has already constituted a political arena to debate the issue of youth in conflict with the law in the presence of public authorities.

The utility of the evaluation varied among the four organizations executing the program. On the one hand it allowed the two stronger organizations to feed the debates held in the political arenas such as the Council on Children and Adolescents, as well as generate visibility for their work. On the other hand, the two organizations that demonstrated greater organizational fragility did not use the evaluation.

FRAMES: A New Methodological Proposal for Qualitative Investigation

Within the scope of the social problem investigated in this evaluation, an important political issue rose from the debate on its main question: What is the life path of the youngsters? The plan was to understand the results fully by means of quantitative investigation. But the goal was to build a methodological repertoire that allowed a comprehensive analysis of the problem, one that goes beyond a reading in which responsibility for the current life status of the youngster who committed an offense would be a causal or linear relationship with the MSE-MA that he or she fulfilled. This problem is a focus for heated debates in the country.

Attempting to get a more comprehensive picture might normally lead to the use of adolescent biographies, and there would be a tendency to appeal to more traditional methods such as individual or focus-group interviews and observations. However, the need to work in four municipalities, with a short period of time for the fieldwork, and the importance of registering the lives of a significant number of youngsters led the evaluation team to think of new techniques to face this situation. It was in this context that the FRAMES (QUADROS) method came to life.

FRAMES consists of 27 drawings (Figure 5.1) that reveal situations that might occur in the lives of youngsters in social-exclusion situations at several levels. These pictures were drawn from debates with youngsters, educators, and bibliographical analysis. They are scenes that allow multiple interpretations and have the power to trigger a dialogue with the youngster. The final pictures were chosen after a trial run was conducted (with eight youngsters, individually) where some frames were discarded and many of them modified. Evidently, the repertoire of scenes ($n = 27$) is limited in relation to the possibilities of a life, and to accommodate unknown possibilities two "joker" pictures were created; that is, totally white or black frames that allow the representation of any situation.

The FRAMES method was used throughout the process of interviewing the youngsters. After completing the questionnaires, youth were invited

Figure 5.1. Examples of Drawings From the FRAMES Method

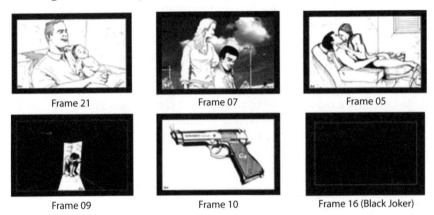

to participate in the FRAMES task, which was administered by anthropologists and psychologists with experience working with youngsters similar to those of the individuals in this evaluation. Young evaluators did not act at this moment. The task was individually administered. All drawings were presented to the youngsters (on the floor, on a desk, wherever there was enough space available) and conversation began with questions such as "what catches your eye?" or "which drawing do you relate to?" In this manner a dialogue began, the main purpose of which was to learn about points on the life path of young offenders. Conversation was stimulated by the drawings; however, it could take any direction established at the meeting between the interviewer and youngster. After every association made by the youngster guided by the drawings, the pictures were readopted to search for new elements and search for new meanings. Thirty administrations of FRAMES were conducted and all the drawings were referred to—narratives used from 2 to 16 drawings and the administration time lasted between 40 minutes and 5 hours.

The FRAMES method proved to be a useful tool in evaluation processes linked to the issue in question, but it can be adapted as a pedagogical instrument to be used by educators who work with this population. The FRAMES method is not, and is not intended to be, a psychological test. Rather, it is a device for mediating dialogue. Out of the total number of administrations, nine stories were chosen for more in-depth analysis, with a reading that seeks to recognize the particularity of each individual life and at the same time seeks to recognize common universal experiences.

The drawings that compose FRAMES have been reproduced and distributed to professionals in Brazil who work with youngsters in risk situations. They have been useful to the field of evaluation but also well beyond it, for example, having an influence on care practices for excluded youngsters. There are records of several different types of applications that range from individual or group interviews to interviews with hearing-challenged youngsters, efforts in the fine arts, the elaboration of comics, and elsewhere. According to reports from these professionals the materials have contributed to the building of dialogue with these youngsters.

References

Brandão, D. B. (2007). *Avaliação com intencionalidade de aprendizagem: Contribuições teóricas para o campo da avaliação de programas e projetos sociais* (Unpublished master's dissertation). Pontificate University, São Paulo, Brasil.

Dussel, E. (2002). *Ética da Libertação na idade da globalização e da exclusão* (2nd ed.). Petrópolis, Brasil: Vozes.

Freire, P. (1996). *Pedagogia do oprimido* (17th ed.). São Paulo, Brasil: Paz e Terra.

Gong, J., & Wright, D. (2007). The context of power—Young people as evaluators. *American Journal of Evaluation, 28*(3), 327–333.

Guba, E., & Lincoln, Y. (1989). *Fourth generation evaluation.* Thousand Oaks, CA: Sage.

Horsch, K., Little, P.M.D., Smith, J. C., Goodyear, L., & Harris, E. (2002). Youth involvement in evaluation and research. *Issues and Opportunities in Out-of-School Time Evaluation, 1.*

House, E., & Howe, K. (1999). *Values in evaluation and social research.* Thousand Oaks, CA: Sage.

Kaplan, A. (2005). *Artistas do invisível: O processo social e o profissional de desenvolvimento.* São Paulo, Brasil: Ed. Peirópolis e Instituto Fonte.

Waiselfisz, J. J. (2004). *Mapa da violência IV: Os jovens do Brasil.* Brasília, Brazil: Unesco, Instituto Ayrton Senna, Ministério da Justiça/ SEDH.

Walker, K. (2007). Youth empowerment evaluation—Learning voice. *American Journal of Evaluation, 28*(3), 321–326.

Whitmore, E., & McKee, C. (2001). Six street youth who could . . . In P. Reason & H. Bradbury (Eds.), *Handbook of action research* (pp. 297–303). Thousand Oaks, CA: Sage.

DANIEL BRAGA BRANDÃO *is an evaluator at MOVE, São Paulo, Brazil.*

ROGÉRIO RENATO SILVA *is an evaluator at MOVE, São Paulo, Brazil.*

RENATA CODAS *is an attorney and project assistant at Fonte Institute, São Paulo, Brazil.*

Letichevsky, A. C., & Penna Firme, T. (2012). Evaluating with at-risk communities:
Learning from a social program in a Brazilian slum. In S. Kushner & E. Rotondo (Eds.),
Evaluation voices from Latin America. New Directions for Evaluation, 134, 61–76.

6

Evaluating With At-Risk Communities: Learning From a Social Program in a Brazilian Slum

Ana Carolina Letichevsky, Thereza Penna Firme

Abstract

This chapter describes a 2-year evaluation of a social program in a Brazilian slum troubled by poverty, unemployment, drug-related threats, and violence, where self-protecting attitudes have led to inhabitant behaviors of fear and silence. Evaluation experience in this unique environment taught us how not to conduct evaluations. Our strategies made more sense where they were informed by what not to do. Trust building as the basis for data collection and data utilization was of utmost importance. Inclusion and empowerment ensured key community member involvement, stakeholder safety and integrity, and just as important, data quality. Emphasis on appreciative inquiry facilitated utilization of findings for community betterment. The significant lesson that emerged astonished the program staff, sponsors, evaluators, and evaluees alike: Evaluation became meaningful to this community. ©Wiley Periodicals, Inc., and the American Evaluation Association.

Resumen

Este documento describe el aprendizaje de una evaluación de dos años de un programa social en un barrio pobre de Brasil preocupado por la pobreza, el desempleo, la amenaza de drogas, y la violencia relacionados, donde la actitud de auto protección han dado lugar a comportamientos de miedo y silencio, por parte de los habitantes. La experiencia de evaluación en este entorno único, nos enseña a cómo no realizar las evaluaciones. Se concluye que el fomento de la confianza es la base para la recopilación y la utilización de los datos. Inclusión y el empoderamiento aseguran la participación clave de miembros de la comunidad, la seguridad y la integridad de las partes interesadas y tan importante: la calidad de los datos. Énfasis en investigación apreciativa de los resultados facilitó el uso del estudio para el mejoramiento de la comunidad. La lección importante que surgió sorprendió al personal del programa, los patrocinadores, los evaluadores y evaludospor igual: la evaluación se hizo significativa para esta comunidad. ©Wiley Periodicals, Inc., and the American Evaluation Association.

Many developing countries are seriously affected by social inequalities. Furthermore, social scenarios are so complex that it is possible to propose completely inappropriate solutions, as the apparent cues of poverty could be disguising deeper aspects that actually deserve more attention (Penna Firme & Letichevsky, 2007). In addition, today's world is going through a crisis of moral and ethical values that affects the structure of society and its educational, social, corporate, and other organizations. This crisis of values is a worldwide problem that appears more or less emphatically in different countries and in different sectors, and seeking and finding strategies to meet this crisis is a task of citizens all around the world (Serpa, Penna Firme, & Letichevsky, 2005).

Generally, this task is more complicated in developing countries, where there is a lack of educational opportunities, governmental processes need more transparency, and democracy is not always implemented in a conscious and responsible way. Although ambitious, there is reason to believe that evaluation can help create new realities as long as it is present in the different sectors of society and counts on multidisciplinary teams of competent professionals.

For the development of a truly evaluative process one needs, among other aspects (a) understanding and respecting the values of the people involved in the process, (b) defining a criterion of excellence, and (c) revealing strengths (which must be preserved and reinforced) and weaknesses (which must be overcome). However, in a developing country with many social needs and demands, the first challenge to building an evaluative culture may be showing that a certain amount of resources must be used to evaluate actions, not just social programs. In other words, we need to explain to people the importance of evaluation as a means of improving the quality of actions, minimizing waste, and maximizing social betterments.

This chapter talks about evaluation of social programs in Brazil through the presentation and discussion of a concrete case: the activities of a slum improvement community program and its accompanying evaluation by a nonprofit organization in Brazil. It is believed that this experiment, which has

NEW DIRECTIONS FOR EVALUATION • DOI: 10.1002/ev

already been replicated in Brazil, might be extrapolated to other developing countries because of the similarities of the social problems that are faced.

The Brazilian Context

Brazil is a large country. It is important to point out that, with the arrival of the Portuguese some 500 years ago, a developing new Portuguese–Iberian–European culture was superimposed on the native Brazilian cultures—a new culture that absorbed the old and ultimately modified it. Later, with slavery, our culture was also highly influenced by African immigrants. Following three centuries under the rule of Portugal, Brazil became an independent nation in 1822 and a Republic in 1889. After a military coup in 1964, which abolished civil rights and reduced social initiatives to a bare minimum, Brazil had a series of military governments. It was only in 1989 that the country returned to a democracy, when the country had direct democratic elections. This new situation was met with a population not entirely prepared for its demands, especially due to a historical lack of importance given to high-quality universal education (Dannemann, Penna Firme, & Letichevsky, 2005). This picture has changed in recent years. Access to high school, after a compulsory nine years, is now universal. However, due to a low percentage of students concluding elementary school, we still have not reached universal outcomes.

The last two decades in Brazil have been characterized by significant efforts in educational and social programs, both in governmental and nongovernmental sectors. Evaluations of these programs are indispensable, but not easy. Brazil is well known for its social inequalities and their perverse consequences. The media, although fulfilling well their role of spreading the news, have been portraying this scenario harshly, perhaps putting excessive weight on problems rather than on solutions. This emphasis has resulted in a state of social panic and near hopelessness for the urban population, especially in large cities, where the problem acquires enormous proportions. Paradoxically, the frequency of violent episodes has created a distortion, where perverse behaviors are seen as trivial. More seriously, those who live in areas of high social risk face tragedies next door and within their home, not just in the media.

In this sense, two parallel cultures coexist in this environment of near panic. Evaluators who often do not live in high-risk areas need to be sensitive and empathetic to understand the cultural codes, signs, and unobtrusive measures. A unique characteristic of this context is the law of silence, in which inhabitants are not allowed to talk about particular events occurring in this environment. First of all, they might be severely punished by those who control the community, albeit illegitimately, if they reveal what should not be known by the constituted authorities. Secondly, community inhabitants feel the need to preserve their identity and dignity.

Brazilian evaluation, therefore, faces a variety of demands from a complex sociopolitical context, and has to accomplish the role often without the benefit of specialist preparation or conditions conducive to evaluation work. One way of addressing this problem is to have other professionals learn evaluation as they develop it as a practice. The principal challenge to the field of evaluation is training professionals in democratic practice, making sure that the knowledge and experience they generate reaches all those involved and interested in developing and improving the quality of what they are evaluating (Penna Firme & Letichevsky, 2002). Metaevaluations are crucial to assure not only the quality of evaluation, but also the quality of evaluation capacity building.

This chapter focuses on the joint action of a community development program and its evaluation in a slum area of Rio de Janeiro, Brazil, with a population of more than 2,000 people. The Betting on the Future program targets an area that includes four extremely poor communities (Parque André Rebouças, Vila Santa Alexandrina, Paula Ramos, and Escadaria) severely affected by violence, mainly caused by drug dealing, which imposed great risks both on collecting data and giving information. The evaluation was conducted by the Cesgranrio Foundation, a nonprofit organization located near the target communities, with the mission of promoting innovation in evaluation theory, methodology, and practice. The Foundation's main purpose is to contribute to social and economic development, aimed at improving the quality of life of those communities. This joint action helped guarantee overall excellence of the work, in a collaborative format. Emphasis was also placed on self-determination, social justice, capacity building, and transformation.

The Betting on the Future Program

In 2003, while developing the idea of a social program in the four communities previously mentioned, key questions were identified: What are the characteristics of the target population? What are the priority needs of the target population? What is the best way to implement the program's actions? When does the evaluation team need to be involved in the process?

A situation analysis was conducted to help answer these questions, a procedure that generated an overall view of each community in terms of their needs, growth opportunities, potential, and limitations. In so doing it was possible to obtain basic information about the communities, such as the number of persons in each community, their home status, years of schooling, occupations and profession, as well as specific information about the needs of different segments in each community. At the end of the situation analysis it was already possible to see the complexity of the target communities and some of the difficulties that would be faced during implementation, as well as potential risks (Fundação Cesgranrio, 2003).

NEW DIRECTIONS FOR EVALUATION • DOI: 10.1002/ev

Information provided by the situation analysis helps in describing the communities. Heads of households are equally divided between men and women and they are mostly Brazilian, born in the city of Rio de Janeiro. They have been living for at least 20 years in the communities, although they were not born there. Some are married and some simply live together. They live in their own houses which are usually built with bricks, have four or more rooms, running water, and sewage. Most have completed elementary school, work, and earn up to two minimum wages, although very few have formal jobs. Most of them do not have health insurance and do not do voluntary work. Some have been exposed to some kind of culture and have been to theatres or museums.

Most of the target families have one to three members, and most do not have all their ID documents. They earn up to three minimum wages, most are not assisted by social programs, and very few have at least one family member doing voluntary work. The great majority declare the absence of artists in the family and few members know the history of these communities.

The communities have television and radio and the members practice different sports, mainly soccer. They do not have access to technology, and they are instructed about sexual abuse, family planning, child and adolescent health, old age, sexuality, nutrition, prenatal care, computer skills, mechanics, secretarial skills, tourism, and foreign languages. They lack day care centers, preschools and schools in general, police stations, health care centers, labor information center, and professional training courses, among others. They also complain about the scarcity of opportunities offered in the communities. However, they are positive about the quality of the church, soccer team, and neighborhood associations.

This information established program priorities including civil documentation; attention to children ages zero to three; professional qualification; supply of cultural, sports, and leisure activities; and preventative action toward children and adolescents. In 2004, the program Betting on the Future was designed based on the assumption that social programs could promote upward social mobility and transform the social reality of communities, and that they should be monitored and evaluated to guarantee that implementation went according to plan. In 2004, we searched for institutional partners to design and implement the program's actions collaboratively with target communities. A number of such partners participated in the overall program.

The Child and Youth Courts, and government agencies in charge of issuing civil documentation, as well as other organizations, all experienced in mobilization actions, served the local population by issuing birth and marriage certificates, and by initiating legal procedures for adoption and custody.

To focus attention on children aged zero to three, the World Organization of Pre-School Education (OMEP), Rio de Janeiro Section, designed and implemented a project that created a group of mothers that would become an awareness-generating center within the community. The group would highlight the relevance of attention to children at this age level, trying to replicate in the communities the notion of child rights. The main achievement of this effort was a petition developed by the mothers demanding the installation of a day care center within the community. In addition to that, several courses have been developed based on the community mothers' requests. A toy center was also built that operated within the neighbors' association.

The XEROX Institute developed a digital inclusion project to respond to the communities' principal demand for professional qualification. It was delivered in two modalities: one devoted to children and adolescents, with an educational focus, and the other to adults to provide access to the digital world. The XEROX Institute proposed a project for the provision of cultural, sports and leisure activities for all age levels. The project includes 17 different sports, including gymnastics for elders, volleyball, adult gymnastics, "capoeira," court soccer (men and women), and other activities such as film screenings followed by debates, storytelling, dramatizing readings, popular dance theme workshops, poetry, popular percussion, theater, choir, and recreation.

AMAR Beneficent Association, a nongovernmental organization (NGO), designed and implemented a project for preventive actions toward children and adolescents involving a two-hour-long extracurricular activity, a snack time, play activities, lectures, and trips. The communities were very conscious that most social and personal high-risk situations involving children and adolescents occurred during the time they were not attending school, because of the lack of any other type of activity, which was clearly demonstrated by the situational analysis. This problem resulted in early pregnancy, drug abuse, participation in criminal activities, and child labor, in short, in the varied risk situations that are well known to us.

Several adjustments have been made to the program along the way, in terms of improving the practice in response to evaluation results. An example of this was the creation of a community newspaper.

The development of the program aims at promoting sustainable gains concerning the community's quality of life. To have a successful program both in terms of attaining objectives and sustaining results, in 2004, two parallel teams were created, one for program monitoring and the other for the external evaluation. Monitoring was implemented throughout the development of the program to inform implementation, although because it was distinct from the evaluation, it made no value judgments. The external evaluation process itself had to be accurate and timely, but subtle, with the right people approached at the right time, and with care taken to ensure no violence was experienced by the evaluators or the community circle. Furthermore, to ensure the quality of the evaluation process, a metaevaluation was also planned. Both evaluation and metaevaluation were conducted by Cesgranrio Foundation.

NEW DIRECTIONS FOR EVALUATION • DOI: 10.1002/ev

The Evaluation of Betting on the Future

Complex issues attend the evaluation of social programs in impoverished social contexts. Sometimes there is an inappropriate conception of the evaluative process, and sometimes evaluations are conducted without sensitivity. Another potential concern has been the distorted use of evaluation findings, which has sometimes damaged efforts made to resolve significant social problems that affect our society. Evaluation in these social contexts should address the following challenges:

- How should social programs and projects be judged?
- How do we ascertain the best use of the resources?
- How can evaluations enlighten ways that lead to a better use of results?
- How do we create reliable information useful for those who make decisions, those who work directly in the programs, and those who theorize their practice?
- How can we avoid potentially useful reports being set aside?
- How do we assure the ethics process?

Clearly, there are no universal answers to such questions; it is not possible to identify the best evaluative approach for all contexts. An evaluation can be introduced in different contexts and, thereby, serve diverse purposes. It should always arrive at a judgment of the merit and the relevance of its object, depending on the needs, dilemmas, and aims of those who are affected by its results.

We can learn from evaluation that is both sensitive and competent in its context and be enlightened by such practice. In this case, the evaluation team sought to integrate a suite of evaluation models focused around inclusive (Mertens, 2003), appreciative (Preskill & Catsambas, 2006), and responsive (Stake, 2004) approaches. The purpose was to have an external view of the overall programming in order to portray the quality as well as the possible limitations and the anxieties and opinions of the beneficiaries. Thus, the evaluation documented the particularities of the program, serving as an evaluation historian (Cronbach, 1980) when we describe and interpret the singular day-to-day process of each focused scenario.

As true evaluations (Stufflebeam & Shinkfield, 1985) require quality information, extensive effort was put into creating and maintaining an environment of confidence and trust. The first step was to include all stakeholders (program staff, beneficiaries, family members, and key people from the community) in the design. It was also necessary to conceive a discrete method to get closer to the community in question. Although the evaluation team had experience of social program evaluation, and poor communities in Brazil suffer common problems (e.g., violence, power struggles, lack of attention from public authorities) each is experienced in a unique way. Throughout, we maintained an appreciative approach, which essentially acknowledged values, capabilities, skills, and actions of the target population. An empowerment approach (Fetterman & Wandersman, 2006) was used to enhance self-determination. During its development, the evaluation considered values, concerns, and perceptions of the programs' stakeholders and strove to identify the program's merit and its internal value, and to discover its relevance demonstrated by its results, repercussions, and possible impacts. "Program evaluation creates alternative ways of thinking and talking about society and its purposes, about the relation between people and social institutions" (Kushner, 2000, pp. 39–40).

Because this was an external evaluation, the team was composed of professionals with no direct connection to the program. The advantage gained by this was that we could offer a complementary view to the self-perception of the program stakeholders. The approach used in the external evaluation was inclusive (Mertens, 2003) in that it emphasized the insertion and participation of all communities affected by the decisions based on the evaluation process. This approach was active in all steps of the evaluation process. In this context, the role of the evaluator was a proactive one in the sense of intervening to change conditions that create social injustice.

Concretely, after understanding the communities' needs and the programs themselves, the starting point for the evaluation team was constructing the evaluative questions as follows:

- To what extent is the project being developed efficiently? (Merit)
- What is the evidence of impact on beneficiaries and communities at large in respect of the improvement of the quality of life? (Impact or Worth)

The next step was immersion in the programs and, in order to look for evidence of merit and impact, the evaluation team constructed social indicators to build the bridge between the observed data and the evaluative questions (Penna Firme, Tijiboy, & Stone, 2001). When a set of indicators had been elaborated, it was possible to establish the criteria to judge what was worthy and what was not, that is, the criteria of excellence would assess results with regard to each indicator. The indicators and their respective criteria of excellence were listed, taking into consideration that results could be achieved at different times. For this reason, a logic model (Frechtling, 2007) was used to describe the connections between the activities carried out in different stages of program implementation, and the expected results in short, medium, and long terms. The indicators were organized into 12 categories, 3 of merit and 9 of impact. Figure 6.1 presents the indicators of merit and impact according to the category, as well as the techniques of data collection in each case, with the respective respondents.

The data were collected from three different sources: (a) beneficiaries (children, youngsters, and adult participants of the program), (b) partners (institutions in charge of program development), and (c) community members. Diverse instruments for data collection were adopted to capture this

Figure 6.1. Criteria, Indicators, and Instrumentation Used in the Evaluation of Betting on the Future

CATEGORY	INDICATORS	Checklist			Focus Group			Interviews		Unobtrusive Measures			Storytelling
		B	P	C	B	P	C	P	C	B	P	C	B
(A) OF IMPACT													
I PERSONAL DEVELOPMENT	Self-esteem												
	Respect for moral values												
	Solidarity												
	Respect for sexuality												
	Life expectancy												
	Respect for rights and duties												
	Recruting (mobilization)												
	Civil documentation												
II VULNERABILITY	Sexual abuse against children and adolescents												
	Children and adolescents dropped out from the community												
	Teenage pregnancy												
	Drug use												
	Exploitation of children and adolescents												
	Teenagers breaking the law												
	Community violence												
III HEALTH	Health preventive actions												
	Hygiene habits												
	Food quality												
	Level for child mortality												
IV EDUCATION	School level												
	School frequency												
	School achievements												
	Preservation of the environment												
	Use of information												
	Creation of local media												
	Index of permanence in school												
V FAMILY	Family relations												
	Family structure												
VI CULTURE	Frequency to cultural activities												
	Artistic-cultural production												
VII WORK	Income improvement												
	Professional occupation												
VIII SPORT AND LEISURE	Participation in sport and leisure activities												
	Changes arising from sport and leisure												
IX DEVELOPMENT OF THE SOCIAL LOCAL PROJECT	Project valorization												
	Valorization of community buildings												
	Community organizations												
(B) OF MERIT													
X QUALITY OF PROJECT ACTIONS	Health preventive actions												
	Children aid from 0–3 years old												
	Professional capacity												
	Children aid from 7–14 years old												
	Sport, leisure, and culture activities												
	TV rooms												
	Access to information												
XI ENVIRONMENTAL CONDITIONS	Access to the project's activities												
	Sewer conditions												
XI DIVERSIFICATION OF ACTIONS	Actions adaptation												
	Integration on inter-project actions												

* B - Beneficiaries, P - Partners, C - Community

reality subtly: three checklists (Stufflebeam, 2001) were developed to be used with partners, beneficiaries, and community; focus groups (Krueger, 1988; Krueger & Casey, 2000) were conducted with representatives of all program participants and community; interviews; unobtrusive measures (Webb, Campbell, Schwartz, & Sechrest, 1966) were utilized to collect spontaneous evidences of merit and impact; and storytelling (Labont & Feather, 1996). The checklists and interviews were pretested in real conditions, which led to changes not only in data-collection instruments, but also in the collection procedures. After the changes, a specialized team and community members generated the data. An essential aspect of methodological development was continuous feedback to all stakeholders with the use of diverse forms of communication to assure the appropriate language was used with different audiences.

To guarantee timely feedback, as data were collected with each instrument, reports were written corresponding to the results framework. Meetings were also conducted to discuss concerns, update information, and build capacity in evaluation. In addition, triangulation was used to integrate information from different sources, techniques, and instruments, a process through which indicators were revised. The next step was the interpretation of results based on the criteria of excellence to answer the evaluative questions.

Validation

Validation of evaluative questions, indicators, criteria, instruments, and results were conducted among beneficiaries and partners during the evaluation process. We emphasized agreement between the evaluation team and the community to assure that the community was always the first audience to receive findings. Co-ownership of the evaluation was the goal. To assure the quality of the evaluation a metaevaluation was conducted according to the guidelines that have been defined and specified by the Joint Committee on Standards for Educational Evaluation (1994). A formative metaevaluation was used for the improvement of the target evaluation. Continuous interaction involving participants and the evaluation team fostered the construction of an evaluation culture in the community, in which community members became critical users capable not only of understanding the results, but also applying them. In this sense, a culture of evaluation supported the development of human and social community capital.

The distinctive aspects of this experience were (a) giving due recognition to the community's knowledge for expressing its own needs, strengths, and priorities as well as raising its expectations for improvement instead of calling an external expert to identify needs and design the program; (b) forming effective partnerships to implement the program activities and to conduct the evaluation and metaevaluation; (c) emphasis on partnerships and community capacity to build evaluations; (d) using evaluation to promote community social justice, transformation, and self-sustainability; and (e) giving continuous feedback to partners, evaluation teams, sponsors, and communities as well as helping to understand and use each result.

Main Results and Lessons Learned

After four years of evaluation, the program has grown, demonstrating positive changes in behavior, attitudes, and habits of beneficiaries and community members, as well as competent and effective accomplishment of program activities (Fundação Cesgranrio, 2006a, 2006b, 2007). In other words, its merit and impact have shown improvement, though there remains a long path to be walked.

Impact

Favorable changes were noted in data from all the sources regarding the following indicators: self-esteem, respect for moral values, respect for sexuality, life expectations, preventive health care, hygiene habits, use of information, school attendance, family relationships, family structure, artistic and cultural production, and participation in leisure and sport activities.

But there were paradoxes, too, which require further investigation. For example, we noted a decrease in mobilization, fewer new local media were created, and a diminished opinion of the program by partners as well as the community. The community pointed out the need to improve newspapers and local radio. The partners indicated the need to improve local information flow. The program partners pointed out that the program was less valued by beneficiaries, which was consistent with the decrease in the proportion of people who have interest in creating new opportunities. The percentage of people from the community who go to community organizations remained stable with a margin for improvement. On the other hand, there was a decrease in the number of people interested in creating new organizations.

The community partners also called attention to the following: People from the community started to note that social economic differences of contemporary society cannot be solved only by external agents, and to secure gains in quality of life the participation of community numbers is fundamental. This seems to be related to a decrease in school failure in middle schools, enhanced self-esteem of children, adults going back to school, legalization of the marital situation of adults in the community through a group of people involving a judge, a priest, and a pastor, and betterment in the behavior of children, teenagers, and adults.

Merit

No definitive results were found, but some positive findings have to do with the following indicators: health-care preventive actions, service for children up to three years old, sport activities, leisure and culture, and access to information. The merit indicators that presented contradictory results were: health service from 7 to 14 years old and access to the project's activities.

Lessons Learned

Each evaluation stresses the importance of ensuring that evaluators are adequately prepared to choose the most appropriate methods; moreover, they must be prepared to analyze and communicate their findings. Evaluators may select a method appropriately, but fail in its application or analysis; the choice of method, the application, and the analysis are connected, but there may yet be shortcomings in communication in terms of failure to indicate the scope and the limitations of findings, failure to point out sources of errors, failure to inform the level of fidelity of the results, and failing to use adequate language to reach the intended audience. On the other hand, there are evaluators who fail to choose an appropriate method (Serpa et al., 2005) arising from (a) the lack of knowledge about the adequacy, the purposes, and the limitations of each method and (b) the choice of the method coming prior to the formulation of the evaluation questions.

Many lessons were learned from the evaluation of the Betting on the Future project, and we have summarized these in Table 6.1.

Conclusions

It seems a paradox to formulate conclusions about the evaluation of ongoing social programs. Programs are constantly going through challenging transformations in search of a better quality of life for citizens. In this evolving scene, new questions would keep emerging as a priori evaluation questions are being answered, which can create a mismatch in the timeliness of the answers and emergent program information needs. However, all partial results obtained throughout program development as described here, considered relevant at the time, were recorded and delivered to the community as well as to the members of the coordination and evaluation teams with minimum lapse of time. Formative use of these results, which documented benefit to participants, was a key feature of the evaluation.

In this sense, the original questions related to the merit of the program, that is, the efficiency of its procedures and the competence of its main actors, were addressed throughout its course. In this sense, a democratic process of sharing competencies, choices, and decisions has been absorbed by the community, which helped to strengthen the neighborhood association and resulted in the articulation of contributions made by its members in the form of ideas and solutions. The cumulative result was the impact of the program on quality of life in terms of individual and community self-esteem, their respect for moral values, solidarity, and strengthening of citizenship.

A look at recent developments of the program reveals evidence of prolonged impact towards sustainability, reaffirming the significance of the program's mission. It is, in fact, hard to separate the program from the community. It would be difficult to determine which caused the bigger

Table 6.1. The Dos and Don'ts—Lessons From the Betting on the Future Evaluation

Steps	What to Do	What Not to Do
Initial negotiations	Be appreciative of community values. Include representatives of all stakeholders.	Impose the evaluator's opinion. Exclude a community leader. Make agreements that one cannot keep.
Evaluation and metaevaluation team formation	Integrate professionals from different backgrounds. Avoid conflict among team members.	Include a large number of people in the team. Include people not open to updating their knowledge and practice about evaluation.
Metaevaluation	Evaluate the evaluation according to the standards. Define criteria to judge achievement of standards. Conduct metaevaluation formatively and summatively.	Consider the evaluative process self-sufficient with no need for self-reflection. Suppress critical comments that help improve the evaluation process.
Negotiations with interested parties	Identify emergent stakeholders. Make sure negotiations coincide with timelines for program decision making.	Make individual decisions without considering the participation of others. Negotiate with people whose ideas and interests are not pertinent to the program.
Involvement of potential users and other interested parties	Identify potential users of program results. Search for other possible users to guarantee sustainability of program results.	Ignore potential users beyond immediate stakeholders. Develop the evaluative process without locating the potential users.
Construction and validation of evaluative questions	Discuss the significance of questions among interested parties. Construct questions related to merit and impact.	Leave the evaluative questions exclusively as the responsibility of the evaluation team. Construct too many questions where the evaluators cannot answer them all.
Creation of an indicators bank	Create indicators in line with evaluative questions. Construct indicators clearly understood by people involved in the program, including community members.	Create indicators after elaborating instruments. Work with predetermined indicators that cannot be changed in line with program development.

(Continued)

Table 6.1. (Continued)

Steps	What to Do	What Not to Do
Construction of criteria for excellence	Define criteria for excellence objectively and in plain language. Justify the definition of criteria of excellence.	Create criteria without participation of stakeholders. Define ambiguous criteria of excellence.
Construction of the data collection instruments	Utilize a range of instruments for data collection. Validate instruments before use.	Construct instruments ignoring the indicators. Use instruments without pretest. Use jargon that is understandable to the evaluation team but not to the respondents.
Data collection	Include community people to help monitor data collection. Include trained people to collect data.	Ignore unexpected information. Utilize data without conducting a critical analysis.
Analysis, processing, and data tabulation	Organize data before analysis. Utilize analysis techniques appropriate to the evaluative questions. Document procedures of analysis and tabulation to allow others to work with the data.	Utilize inadequate analysis techniques that are not compatible with the sample and/or with the evaluation approach. Construct tables and figures that are not going to be used.
Data triangulation	Integrate different observers, techniques, and sources to validate data. Repeat the triangulation process wherever necessary.	Ignore divergent information. Incorporate data without discussion.
Results interpretation	Keep the interpretation linked to evaluation questions. Take into consideration the possible limitations of time, methodological procedures, and scope. Emphasize positive findings before negative ones.	Interpret results without justification. Suppress positive or negative findings. Disseminate findings before revealing them to community members and program people.
Preliminary report	Utilize appropriate language to explain intentions, procedures, results, and recommendations. Assure timeliness of the report.	Resist negotiation and amendment of findings. Leave unanswered questions in the report. Produce an overly long report.
Validation of the preliminary report	Involve all stakeholders in the process of validation. Incorporate stakeholder suggestions to the report.	Exclude stakeholders. Make changes in the report without giving reasons.
Final report	Make a report in an appropriate length so it can be absorbed by potential users. Include an executive summary.	Write a report that only professional evaluators can understand. Include information beyond the scope of the evaluation, especially information that can invade the privacy of the community.

impact on the other, the community or the program. Nowadays there is a strong partnership between the community and the program, in such a way that the community members visit homes in a systematic way, to inform about the program's actions and to collect information necessary for the evaluation, recognizing its importance for the community's developmental process. The evaluation has become part of that process and can claim having made a contribution to a significant decrease in illiteracy, gains in environmental preservation, enhanced subjective well-being of children, more activities for youth, access to cultural events, professional qualification, the right to come and go, and higher levels of community safety and stability.

References

Cronbach, L., & Associates. (1980). *Towards reform of program evaluation*. San Francisco, CA: Jossey-Bass.

Dannemann, A. C., Penna Firme, T., & Letichevsky, A. C. (2005). Setting up the Brazilian evaluation network: A challengling work with no boundaries. *Revista Ensaio: Avaliação e Políticas Públicas em Educação, Rio de Janeiro, Brasil, 13*(19), 515–533.

Fetterman, D., & Wandersman, A. (Eds.). (2006). *Empowerment evaluation–Principles in practice*. New York, NY: The Guilford Press.

Frechtling, J. A. (2007). *Logic modeling methods in program evaluation*. San Francisco, CA: Wiley.

Fundação Cesgranrio. (2003). *Análise situacional das comunidades envolvidas no projeto de desenvolvimento social local: Relatório final*. Rio de Janeiro, Brasil: Fundação Cesgranrio.

Fundação Cesgranrio. (2006a). *Projeto Apostando no Futuro: Relatório referente à comparação entre a 1ª e a 2ª checklist* (unpublished report). Rio de Janeiro, Brasil: Fundação Cesgranrio.

Fundação Cesgranrio. (2006b). *Projeto Apostando no Futuro: Relatório referente aos grupos focais* (unpublished report). Rio de Janeiro, Brasil: Fundação Cesgranrio.

Fundação Cesgranrio. (2007). *Projeto Apostando no Futuro: Informe parcial de avaliação* (unpublished report). Rio de Janeiro, Brasil: Fundação Cesgranrio.

Joint Committee on Standards for Educational Evaluation. (1994). *The program evaluation standards* (2nd ed.). Thousand Oaks, CA: Sage.

Krueger, R. (1988). *Developing questions for focus groups*. Thousand Oaks, CA: Sage.

Krueger, R., & Casey, M. A. (2000). *Focus groups: A practical guide for applied research*. Thousand Oaks, CA: Sage.

Kushner, S. (2000). *Personalizing evaluation*. Thousand Oaks, CA: Sage.

Labont, R., & Feather, J. (1996). *Handbook on using stories in health promotion practice*. Ottawa, Canada: Minister of Supply and Services.

Mertens, D. M. (2003). The inclusive view of evaluation: Visions for the new millennium. In S. I. Donaldson & M. Scriven (Eds.), *Evaluating social programs and problems. Visions for the new millennium*. Englewood Cliffs, NJ: Lawrence Erlbaum.

Penna Firme, T., & Letichevsky, A. C. (2002). O desenvolvimento da capacidade de avaliação no século XXI: Enfrentando o desafio através da meta-avaliação. *Ensaio: Avaliação e Políticas Públicas em Educação, Rio de Janeiro, Brasil, 10*(30), 289–300.

Penna Firme, T., & Letichevsky, A. C. (2007). Improved community condition in a Brazilian slum: A significant consequence of its evaluation. *Ensaio: Avaliação e Políticas Públicas em Educação, Rio de Janeiro, Brasil, 15*(55), 299–310.

Penna Firme, T., Tijiboy, J. A., & Stone, V. I. (2001). Avaliação de programas sociais: Como enfocar e como pôr em prática. Rio do Janeiro, Brasil: Mimeografado.

Preskill, H. S., & Catsambas, T. T. (2006). *Reframing evaluation through appreciative inquiry*. Thousand Oaks, CA: Sage.

Serpa, C. A., Penna Firme, T., & Letichevsky, A. C. (2005). Ethical issues of evaluation practice within the Brazilian political context. *Ensaio: Avaliação e Políticas Públicas em Educação, Rio de Janeiro, 13*(46), 105–114.

Stake, R. E. (2004). *Standards-based and responsive evaluation*. Thousand Oaks, CA: Sage.

Stufflebeam, D. L. (2001). Evaluation checklists: Practical tools for guiding and judging evaluation. *American Journal of Evaluation, 22*(1), 71–79.

Stufflebeam, D. L., & Shinkfield, A. S. (1985). *Systematic evaluation: A self institutional guide to theory and practice*. Dordrecht, Holland: Kluwer-Nijhoff.

Webb, E. J., Campbell, D. T., Schwartz, R. D., & Sechrest, Z. B. (1966). *Unobtrusive measures: Nonreactive research in the social sciences*. Chicago, IL: Rand McNally.

ANA CAROLINA LETICHEVSKY *is superintendent of the Academic Department, Cesgrangrio Foundation, Rio do Janeiro, Brazil.*

THEREZA PENNA FIRME *works as the Evaluation Center coordinator, Cesgrangio Foundation, Rio do Janeiro, Brazil.*

NEW DIRECTIONS FOR EVALUATION • DOI: 10.1002/ev

Cunill-Grau, N., & Ospina, S. M. (2012). Performance measurement and evaluation systems: Institutionalizing accountability for governmental results in Latin America. In S. Kushner & E. Rotondo (Eds.), *Evaluation voices from Latin America. New Directions for Evaluation, 134*, 77–91.

7

Performance Measurement and Evaluation Systems: Institutionalizing Accountability for Governmental Results in Latin America

Nuria Cunill-Grau, Sonia M. Ospina

Abstract

Results-based performance measurement and evaluation (PME) systems are part of a global current in public administration. In the Latin American context, this trend is also a reflection of the broader processes of reform of the latter half of the 20th century, including the modernization of public administration, as well as broad processes of decentralization and democratization, both of which are dimensions of development in Latin America, regardless of the political and ideological orientation of specific governments. This chapter documents the development of such evaluative approaches to organizational quality and raises some issues for further discussion. ©Wiley Periodicals, Inc., and the American Evaluation Association.

Resumen

La medición de resultados del desempeño y los sistemas de evaluación (PME) son parte de una corriente mundial en la administración pública. En el contexto de América Latina, esta tendencia es también un reflejo de los procesos más amplios de la reforma de la segunda mitad del siglo 20, incluyendo la modernización de la administración pública, así como amplios procesos de descentralización y democratización—ambas dimensiones del desarrollo en la región, independientemente de la orientación política e ideológica de sus gobiernos. Este artículo documenta el desarrollo de tales métodos de evaluación de calidad de la organización y plantea varias cuestiones. ©Wiley Periodicals, Inc., and the American Evaluation Association.

The emphasis on results through performance measurement and evaluation (PME) systems in Latin America is promoted as a vehicle for greater transparency and efficiency of government action. As such, it is a means toward improving the state's ability to have an impact on collective goals. This discussion is based on the comparative study undertaken by the authors, in the framework of the CLAD–World Bank Project "Strengthening of Monitoring and Evaluation Systems in Latin America," developed in 12 countries between December 2006 and October 2007 (Cunill-Grau & Ospina Bozzi, 2008). We aimed to explore the advances and the challenges experienced by these 12 nations (see Table 7.1), focusing on PME systems that encompass a cross section of government work, not only that of a particular agency. Our goal was to contribute to illuminating the factors affecting the process and level of institutionalization of PME systems in Latin America. This goal is increasingly relevant. Many developing nations have begun to implement PME systems, in the best cases within a broader agenda of installing results-oriented public administration (Ospina Bozzi, 2001; Kusek & Rist, 2004). The question arises of how best to understand and study the emerging and past lessons of this process? OECD nations have had over 20 years to implement such systems, but the political, social, and historical context in European countries make it less than realistic as a reference to understand current dynamics in the context of Latin American and other developing economies.

In the Latin American case, empirical studies and knowledge-sharing processes promoted by the World Bank and the Inter-American Development Bank (IDB) have shown substantial advances in the inculcation of PME systems in the region. They have also highlighted the close relationship between these and an agenda to promote results-based public administration. There have been, however, few comparative studies that can identify patterns and generalize lessons from this regional process. Those that exist cover only a few nations taking part in this trend (Cunill-Grau & Ospina Bozzi, 2003; Mackay, 2007; Zaltsman, 2006a, 2006b).

There are a range of tools, models, and functions that comprise each example within the PME systems across Latin America. Understanding this complexity requires a systematic study of multiple analytic factors across the cases (Ospina, 2001). Indeed, the lack of a consensus in the existing literature as to what constitutes a national PME system, and even the very definition and differentiation of the concepts of performance measurement and evaluation has heretofore been a limiting factor.

Our research was designed with the flexibility to capture PME systems at the federal and/or central levels, and to encompass embryonic pockets of

PME implementation as well as robust and overlapping national systems. We also sought to fill the vacuum of wide-ranging analyses in the existing literature by addressing questions of the interaction between PME systems and civil society in Latin America.

Conceptual Framework for Understanding PME in Latin America

We framed the study of PME systems in reference to evaluative capabilities, and within a demand-driven model that focuses on the use of PME systems. This contrasts with a technocratic model, where quality information systems intrinsically justify themselves.

One view of developing evaluative capabilities frames this as an interactive, gradual, and creative process of mutual learning, where subjects (individuals or organizations) improve and complement their knowledge, skills, and attitudes to address situations effectively and in a context-appropriate manner (Rotondo, 2007). Another view holds that this development demands strengthening the ability and will of actors potentially involved to commission, conduct, understand, and use evaluation (Bamberger, Rugh, & Mabry, 2006, p. 356). Both definitions underscore two critical factors of growing importance: the learning process and the range and multiplicity of actors encompassed by evaluation. A supply-driven model to evaluative capabilities implies that the sole purpose of a PME system is to provide a great deal of information about an undertaking, or many quality evaluations. A demand-driven model, in contrast, defines the primary purpose in relation to their utilization for attaining government objectives (Mackay, 2006). Adopting a demand-driven model has two implications: First, it offers a bar to measure success for PME systems (the more they are employed and their information utilized, the more successful they are); and, second, it offers a trajectory (the greater their demand, the greater the probability that they are used). The demand-driven model reinforces a critical link between utility of the PME system and its potential for institutionalization. Focusing analytical attention on the promotion or creation of demand is necessary precisely because it is not often realistic to assume existing demand in the public sector (Toulemonde, 1999, p. 153).

The literature poses several approaches to evaluate the institutionalization of a PME system. Feinstein (1993) proposes four key dimensions of PME: (a) its design (resources, structure, and functions of the system); (b) its results; (c) utility of the products (for project, donor, government personnel, beneficiaries, and anyone else interested); and (d) effective use of contextual environment. Rotondo (2007) focuses on three dimensions: (a) operational framework (enabled human resources, available financial resources, and organizational resources for change management); (b) quality and utility of the products (flexible and appropriate methodologies, participative development, definition of changes, and instruments and indicators used), and (c) use and communication of results through institutionalized avenues for feedback to planning and strategic processes, with dissemination to key actors. For Mackay (2006) institutionalization is understood as the creation of a PME system whose results are positively valued by the principal interested parties, and are employed in the quest for good governance, so long as there exists sufficient demand for the PME function to guarantee its funding and sustainability in the foreseeable future.

In our view, the institutionalization of a PME system goes beyond establishing processes, institutional structures, committees, and other elements allowing for its existence. The degree of institutionalization is reflected in the use of established structures to have a real impact on public administration, using the information generated by the PME systems. This addresses both capabilities and institutional incentives for the use of the information generated, even by those entities being evaluated. Institutionalization also relates to the ability of the PME system to withstand political changes.

Overall, the institutionalization of a PME system is less a function of its age, and more a function of factors like the conditions of its emergence and implementation over time, the political and technical interest it receives, and the utility of its findings to potential consumers. Determining the exact degree of institutionalization of each PME system is something of a fool's errand, owing to a lack of hard data that would allow the analysis to move beyond a subjective valuation of the nature and quality of a range of factors that make a system viable in the long term. We have to begin somewhere, however, and our study postulated that institutionalization, as a dependent variable, can be best understood through an examination of its component factors. The four broad categories of such factors we chose were: (a) the degree of functional and instrumental diversification, (b) institutional coherence (vertical and horizontal), (c) uses of information, and (d) sustainability. Each is explained when presenting the findings.

Methodology

Given the many attempts at PME in Latin America, some denoted as systems of national scope, we asked to what degree the capacity for PME has been institutionalized in the public sector in Latin America. A comparative analysis of the institutionalization of 16 PME processes in 12 countries in the region helped answer the question (our unit of analysis was the PME system, not the country). We focused on systems that sought to implement a results-oriented evaluation at the national level. Our methodology consisted of formal case studies using primary documents, interviews with a representative sample of 15–25 key actors per country, a common protocol for all cases, and case validation. Local researchers with basic familiarity with the system were chosen to do the country-based fieldwork and write the case.

Stage one of our research focused on individual cases and included developing and validating the protocol, researching and writing the country case studies, sharing drafts and feedback among team members, and having the cases validated by relevant government officials. Stage two focused on comparative analysis, including analyzing and classifying the systems, comparing them by subcategory, developing a comparative narrative, and validating the report. We applied the institutionalization factors outlined in the conceptual framework to each case and then to the cross comparison. These findings reported below are provisional, as most of the systems are in the process of development.

Descriptive Findings

Our initial analysis yielded a classification of the Latin American PME systems into four distinct groups, as summarized in Table 7.1, based on the political, economic, mixed, or social orientation of the PME systems. But within each category we also find important differences. As Schick (2005) suggests, some countries have used primarily the budget as a tool of allocation, whereas other countries have a planning process based on the National Development Plan (NDP). This institutional design affects the traits and functions of PME systems, and also interacts with the determination to opt for predominantly political or economic systems, leading to the particular nature of each system in each nation. Therefore, across the categories, PME systems fell into one of four subcategories, depending on whether they were linked to the NDP in a multifunctional or single-function capacity, or linked to the national budget in either capacity.

A brief examination of Table 7.1 indicates that there are about as many political systems as economic, mixed, or social ones. Moreover, the political orientation is not limited to countries where the PME system is explicitly tied to the NDP, but crosses over into states driven by the national budget. Finally, most systems espouse a multifunctional vocation, which will be discussed below, though oftentimes it is not realized.

Politically oriented PME systems seek to perfect the results of the state's activities aligned to public policies. They often translate into exercises in accountability within the state—for instance, agencies giving accounts to a national authority, cabinet officers to a president, or a president to Congress. These PME systems often also aspire to offer accountability outside the state machine, from the government to civil society and the citizenry. Within this group, some systems had a multifunctional intent. They aspired to improve political decision making, and intended to influence the processes of budgetary allocation, or, at least, generate feedback loops in public institutions. These systems are, after all, directly related to the results of implementing government planning. Even though they may not succeed in realizing this multifunctional aspiration, it identifies the potential. This subcategory

Table 7.1. Analytical Map of PME Systems

	Context of Spending Allocations (at the Country Level)			
	National Development Plan		*National Budget*	
	Functional Vocation		*Functional Vocation*	
System's General Orientation	*Multifunctional*	*Monofunctional*	*Multifunctional*	*Monofunctional*
Predominantly political	• SINASID Nicaragua • SINE Costa Rica • SINERGIA Colombia	• SMMP Brasil	• SERP-Gerencia Honduras • PEG/SEV Uruguay	• SPG Chile
Predominantly economic	• SED México		• SCG Chile • SSEGP Perú • SSEEP Argentina	• MCE-SIPP Paraguay
Explicitly economic and political (mixed)	• PPA Brasil • SE del PND Bolivia (?)			
Predominantly social	• SSEPPS Brasil • Programas Sociales México		• MIDEPLAN Chile • SIEMPRO Argentina	

includes Costa Rica's SINE, Colombia's SINERGIA, and Nicaragua's SINASID. None of these models are mutually exclusive of other PME systems with more focused functions, and in many cases these other systems generate overlaps and contradictory demands on agencies. Nevertheless, it is the function of validating the integrity of the NDP that makes them the core of PME efforts by the respective governments. A second subcategory, including Honduras's and Uruguay's systems, are not based upon a formalized national planning process, but aim to introduce a planning capacity. A third subcategory are systems born with a single function, around a macrostrategic coordination role. These include the presidential objectives of Chile and Brazil.

The main goal of economic-oriented PME systems is to rationalize and optimize public spending, as evidenced by appropriate allocation of human and financial resources in public administration. These systems are integrally linked to, if not rooted in, public budgetary and financial processes. Broad public policies and strategic planning, although relevant in some cases, take a back seat to the cycles of budgetary management. This category can be further broken down into subcategories according to the primary tool of allocation and functional goals. Chile, Peru, Argentina, and Paraguay work around budgeting processes while Mexico has a planning process based on the NDP. These systems almost invariably are managed under the purview of the relevant economic ministries in their respective countries, and particularly their budgetary arms. They are all framed, with varied degrees of intensity, within the context of generating a culture of results-oriented budgeting (ROB) or transitioning from traditional models to results-based budgeting (RBB). RBB implies directly linking budgetary allocations to performance, whereas ROB utilizes performance data as an element in the budgetary allocation process. In either case, the temporal dimension is key, as these processes involve examining the past for at least one fiscal year, the present, and planning for the immediate future (Shack, 2007). (As one might expect, these PME systems are directly linked to other attempts to modernize the fiscal administration of the public sector, like the creation of an Integrated System of Financial Administration, SIAF, and a National System of Public Investment, SNIP, both of which are instruments that have become more common in the region since the 1980s and1990s.)

The only case that clearly constitutes a system of mixed orientation (political and economic) is Brazil's Pluriannual Plan. Nevertheless, given change processes documented in the larger study, it is highly probable that this type will increase over time in the region. We did not explore or analyze the systems categorized as predominantly social, as these were deemed beyond the scope of our study.

Figure 7.1 describes the time line on which these varied systems were developed. Dark gray indicates years of experimentation before creating the formal system. It makes transparent variations associated with the choice to create the full system at once or to grow it incrementally. In some instances

Figure 7.1. Evolution of the PME Systems

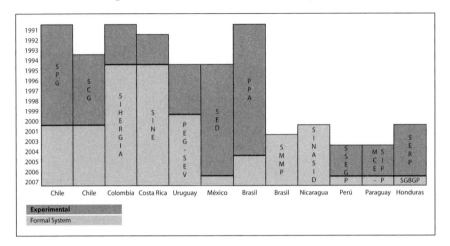

the timing and consequent maturity of systems is critical to understanding differences in otherwise similar PME models. However, neither age nor pace of development explains the level of institutionalization per se.

Analytic Findings

Owing to limitations of space, we will only offer a high-level overview of our detailed findings. For a more comprehensive description of the PME systems and a comparative analysis within and across categories, we encourage the reader to turn to the original study.

Functional and Instrumental Diversification

Analytical factors in this category included the PME's level of action (micro or macro); the monitoring and evaluation instruments used to carry out its functions; the capacity of the system to consolidate and/or diversify the instruments; and, hence, the primary system functions. A key finding was that, although the majority of the PME systems manifested a multifunctional intent, only very few systems realized this in practice. Those that did seemed to have the highest degree of institutionalization. In the case of the SCG of Chile, there is a champion for the system who possesses influence over the entire public sector, namely, the powerful Ministry of Hacienda (Treasury), which seems to have been key in solidifying the multifunctional intent of the system (Mackay, 2006). The consequent diversification of the tools at the disposal of the Chilean system would seem to support this conclusion: The SCG works toward the efficient allocation of expenditure, but also improving the management of public programs and institutions.

NEW DIRECTIONS FOR EVALUATION • DOI: 10.1002/ev

A second example of clear multifunctionality can be seen in Brazil, where the PME system of the Pluriannual Plan effectively supports the function of government planning and the evaluation of budgetary proposals. It is also the only case of a mixed system combining political and economic orientations. Other systems, like Mexico's SED, or the SIERP in Honduras, were in the process of developing tools to manifest their multifunctional vocation, but these remained aspirations at the time of the study. A separate way to enhance the probability of use of PME results is ensuring that they have practical value for a range of users. Enlarging the analysis to encompass this type of diversified function allows the universe of what could be called multifunctional systems to expand somewhat. There emerges a certain correspondence between politically oriented systems and diversification of potential users. The aim of accountability, which characterizes such systems, transforms the citizenry into a potential active agent in shaping policy, as we clearly see formally stated in the SINERGIA system in Colombia, despite the lack of evidence of advances in achieving this goal. A potential consumer of PME results that tended to remain marginal across the board is the leadership stratum of public administration. As such, the managerial learning component of all the PME systems remains a theoretical goal, despite the beginnings of mechanisms to incentivize the attention of these consumers.

A second key finding reinforcing the weakness of the functional diversification concerns the instruments. Evaluation requires analytical tools to obtain the required information to assess causal links between the intervention and its impact. In contrast, monitoring requires collecting information about predetermined performance indicators to follow up the intervention over time.

Monitoring and evaluation are used in one of the two complementary systems found in both Chile and Brazil, as well as in Colombia and Mexico. Nicaragua's SINASID and Uruguay's PEG SEV, however, only use monitoring tools, and Costa Rica, Paraguay, and Honduras had plans to use evaluation tools, but only used monitoring at the time of the study.

Institutional Coherence

This category refers to the system's capacity for integration. Vertical coherence means reciprocal alignment between lower and higher jurisdictions, from supervisory units to agencies, to broader policy sectors; horizontal coherence refers to the PME system's capacity for integration with other key processes like planning, budgeting, and human resources management. Our findings support the argument that higher levels of institutional coherence, both vertical and horizontal, correspond to higher levels of utility, and as such to higher levels of institutionalization. Commonly identified goals and indicators lead to greater vertical coherence, and are facilitated by systems with a political orientation, as in the case of Colombia, Costa Rica,

NEW DIRECTIONS FOR EVALUATION • DOI: 10.1002/ev

Nicaragua, and now Uruguay, as well as in the Presidential Goals monitoring systems of Brazil and Chile. That said, the macrolevel specialization of political systems acts against the likelihood of appropriation of the system by all its component agencies.

In theory, when a system is imposed through a centralized institutional structure, vertical coherence is harder to achieve than it would be when monitoring and evaluation practices are negotiated and agreed upon in ways that increase a sense of ownership of those involved. In this regard, Chile's SCG is an exception, as is the value of the flow of information in both directions, which ensures that the PME products feed back into the managerial levels, and are expressed in commitments to improve public projects and organizations. However, it is clear that in Chile public managers do not participate in the determination of PME priorities and in the definition of management indicators. In contrast, the self-evaluation component of Brazil's Pluriannual Plan would seem to ensure greater levels of appropriation by managerial levels.

In general, we noted interesting advances in the realm of vertical integration in the region. The key would appear to be the political decision in several countries to promote results-oriented public administration. Although no system truly attempts to monitor and evaluate the entire gamut from macro- to microlevels, there are steps in this direction. In some cases this happens within the context of institutionalizing strategic planning in the public sector, and in other cases within the context of a national planning system as expressed through NDPs. We are, indeed, beginning to see stronger definition of objectives and goals and the measurement of execution in relation to these goals—notwithstanding there may be a discussion to be held on the feasibility and utility of tight vertical consensus in any organization.

We found considerable problems in the area of horizontal integration, that is, linkages between PME systems and other processes of the public policy cycle. The situation is not identical to what we noted some years ago (Cunill-Grau & Ospina Bozzi, 2003) but progress is slow. Perhaps more awareness of the limitations of early systems has motivated efforts to link planning and budgeting better. Steps are being taken toward results-oriented budgets, not only in Chile, Brazil, Mexico, and Uruguay, but also in Peru, Honduras, and Argentina, among others. This has been accompanied by a trend toward revaluing the institutionalization of macroplanning processes to achieve a greater government-wide coherence, critically in Peru, Uruguay, and Bolivia. We also note efforts to have PME systems provide information about physical and fiscal execution, denoting an effort at horizontal integration. There is also a clear trend toward achieving a link between planning, budgeting, and PME around development projects.

Notwithstanding these advances, when budgetary processes are too inflexible and not sufficiently coupled with planning processes, this becomes an obstacle to achieving horizontal coherence. Furthermore, systems coordinated by ministries other than Hacienda tend to experience severe problems in communicating with that ministry. There are also great difficulties in countries without institutionalized development plans. A final critical problem in horizontal integration concerns the coordination between various entities that have assigned results-based PME functions. In some cases, like Costa Rica, the laws themselves have caused an overlap of competencies between the Planning Ministry, the Ministry of Hacienda, and the Contraloría. The creation of intersectoral commissions in Brazil, Colombia, Costa Rica, and Chile do not always offer fundamental solutions to this problem. Our analysis also showed the importance of coordination among international organizations to generate greater synergies between the various entities linked to PME in each country. A final key issue is the poor linkages between PME systems and the national statistics offices.

Use of Information

This category refers to the quality and impact of the information produced by the system. The use of information is in large part a function of the PME system's diversification and internal coherence: Greater degrees in these factors correlate to greater use of information, and as such greater demand and institutionalization. Mixed orientation systems and those having accountability as an explicit objective seem to have the best advantages in this regard. There are, however, other key factors worth mentioning.

The first is the limited credibility of the information (both the indicators that serve as inputs to the systems, and the reports generated as outputs). The reasons are varied: The low quality of data submitted to coordinating entities, doubts about the government's ability for self-evaluation, and the unilateral flow of information upwards (in all but SCG in Chile and the Pluriannual Plan in Brazil). Lack of feedback for the providers of information creates a disincentive to take the process seriously in anticipation of receiving useful information down the line.

As Mackay points out (2006), there may be some correlation between the maturity of the PME system and the quality of its information. The PME system associated with Brazil's Pluriannual Plan and Chile's SCG, as well as Mexico's external impact evaluations, would seem to support this thesis, being of greater age and having higher quality information. That said, the Costa Rican case demonstrates that maturity of the system is not a sufficient condition. There also is an interesting halo affect where systems conducting evaluation and monitoring tend to have greater data credibility than those doing only monitoring.

Another factor affecting the use of information is the perspective of the administrations in power, and the level of presidential attention. The cases of the SINE in Costa Rica and SINERGIA in Colombia support this view. However, even in these cases, the evidence is mixed, and nuanced by counterexamples, as the changing nature of the system in some administrations suggests.

Greater utilization of information was also associated with an obligation to relate corrective measures to PME reports, as in Mexico and Chile in the context of external evaluations. For example, in Chile's SCG, formal commitments the evaluated agencies make to implement the recommendations within a given time frame are followed up to ensure compliance. Presence of another fixed consumer, such as the donor community in Nicaragua and Honduras, also generates greater usage of the PME information. We found limited mechanisms for communication and dissemination of the results of PME to the general public, and a waste of the possibilities for participation and control by the citizenry.

It is possible that PME information is being assimilated and used over the longer term in ways we have not captured in our study. Zaltsman (2007) notes the need to differentiate between diverse types of utilization in these systems. Certainly we have seen uses of the information to legitimize decisions taken a priori, as well as a high level of conceptual appropriation with regards to results-based management and to the need to manage the implementation of plans and projects by public administration actors.

Sustainability

This included analysis of the legal framework sustaining the PME system, its financing, and its personnel. We found no clear patterns to determine with any precision the real impact of financing mechanisms and personnel status on the sustainability of systems. In Chile and Colombia, for instance, staff are not permanent, yet the systems are strong. In Colombia the financing of the coordinating unit is external (through international cooperation), yet the system has survived more than four administrations. In several other countries, like Nicaragua, international cooperation may play a major role in sustainability.

Factors mentioned as impacting sustainability (although we could not identify patterns) include the maturity of the system; the technical capabilities of personnel; political leadership, particularly, again, the president's attention; statutory issues, laws that created the PME systems or other related laws (e.g., the Law of Social Development in Mexico); the general institutional framework of the country; PME impact, wherein sustainability is linked to a PME system having real consequences; and last, once again, the synchronization or lack thereof between planning, budgeting, and evaluation.

Conclusions

Mindful of the state of the art with regard to the analysis of the institutionalization of results-based PME systems, our comparison of four key factors offers a starting point for studying this process: functional and instrumental diversification, institutional coherence, uses of the information, and sustainability. Our findings suggest that the use of information, in turn influenced by diversification and coherence factors, seems to be a driving force toward institutionalization, as proposed by a demand-driven model. Furthermore, rather than age, the institutionalization of a PME system seems to be more a function of the conditions of its creation and implementation over time, as well as of the demand for it, based on the utility of its findings to potential consumers, including an informed citizenry.

The state-based trend documented here may be conceptually linked to a parallel development in the region: the emergence of a new generation of NGOs and (politically neutral) Social Observatories specializing in holding the state to public account (Cunill-Grau, 2008). These groups work independently from the State, collecting data or making government information accessible to citizens in order to demand accounts for actions and public resources. As accountability mechanisms, they contrast significantly with the PME systems described in this paper, constructed from inside the State, usually from the executive, for government's direct use. The accountability vocation of these systems nevertheless does suggest great potential for interaction with an active civil society. Indeed, an interaction between State and civil society actors could be productive in broadening accountability and thus democratic governance. This is so because—assuming mutual respect for autonomy between the two parties—an accountability interface could enhance informed action from both parts, perhaps even opening the space for a joint construction of democracy.

However, we did not find evidence in our 2007–2008 study that this potential is being realized. Things might have changed since, and there are some grounds to speculate on the dynamics of a possible convergence of these trends in the region. Be that as it may, the extent of this possibility and its consequences for greater accountability represent only queries in an agenda for future research. A promising question, for example, would explore the institutional and social conditions required to establish this type of productive relationship between the PME systems and the newly organized social practices mentioned above.

Our study goes into considerably more detail than limitations of space would allow us to summarize here, and we encourage the reader to refer to the original report for further information and evidence in support of our conclusions. A key message from our findings is that the institutionalization of PME systems in the region has the potential to make them better tools of democracy and development. Although some evidence suggests movement in the right direction, much more needs to be done to realize this goal.

References

Bamberger, M., Rugh, J., & Mabry, L. (2006). *Realworld evaluation: Working under budget, time, data, and political constraints.* Thousand Oaks, CA: Sage.

CLAD–Banco Mundial. (2007). Fortalecimiento de los sistemas de monitoreo y evaluación (M&E) en América Latina. Informes nacionales referidos a: Argentina (Carlos Canievsky); Bolívia (Azul del Villar); Brasil (Humberto Falcao Martins); Chile (Salvador Ríos Hess); Colombia (Julio Villarreal); Costa Rica (Mario Mora Quirós); Honduras (Manuel Fernando Castro); México (Alejandro Medina Giopp); Nicaragua (Rosa Elizabeth Flores Medina); Paraguay (Josefina Adriana Romero S.); Perú (Nelson Shack); Uruguay (Nora Berretta). Caracas, Venezuela: Centro Latinoamericano de Administración para el Desarrollo, CLAD.

Cunill-Grau, N. (2008). La construcción de ciudadanía desde una institucionalidad pública ampliada. In *Democracia/estado/ciudadanía. Hacia un estado de y para la democracia en América Latina, PNUD, serie contribuciones al debate* (Vol. II, pp. 113–138). Lima, Perú: Sede PNUD.

Cunill-Grau, N., & Ospina Bozzi, S. M. (Eds.). (2003). *Evaluación de resultados para una gestión pública moderna y democrática: Experiencias Latinoamericanas.* Caracas, Venezuela: CLAD; AECI/MAP/FIIAPP.

Cunill-Grau, N., & Ospina Bozzi, S. M. (2008). *Fortalecimiento de los sistemas de monitoreo y evaluación (M&E) en América Latina. Comparative report of 12 countries.* Caracas, Venezuela: Centro Latinoamericano de Administración para el Desarrollo, CLAD and Banco Mundial.

Feinstein, O. N. (1993). *Método para el análisis rápido concentrado de sistemas de seguimiento y evaluación.* Rome, Italy: International Fund for Agricultural Development (FIDA).

Kusek, J. Z., & Rist, R. C. (2004). *Ten steps to a results based monitoring and evaluation system: A handbook for development practitioners, International Bank for Reconstruction and Development.* Washington, DC: World Bank.

Mackay, K. (2006). *Institucionalización de los sistemas de seguimiento y evaluación para mejorar la gestión del sector público.* Washington, DC: World Bank.

Mackay, K. (2007). *How to build M&E systems to support better government.* Washington, DC: World Bank.

Ospina Bozzi, S. (2001). La evaluación de la gestión pública: Conceptos y aplicaciones en América Latina. *Reforma y Democracia, 19,* 89–122.

Rotondo, E. L. (2007, July). *¿Cómo instituir la capacidad en seguimiento y evaluación?: Lecciones aprendidas en el desarrollo de la capacidad evaluativa para la lucha contra la pobreza rural de un programa regional.* Presentation to ReLAC Second Conference Aportes del Seguimiento y la Evaluación a la Gobernabilidad y Democracia, Bogotá, Colombia.

Schick, A. (2005). *Una agenda para la gestión presupuestaria: Un documento conceptual para establecer una red de gestión presupuestaria en la región de América Latina y el Caribe.* Washington, DC: Interamerican Development Bank.

Shack, N. (2007). *Fortalecimiento de los sistemas de monitoreo y evaluación (M&E) en América Latina. National report.* Caracas, Venezuela: Centro Latinoamericano de Administración para el Desarrollo, CLAD, World Bank.

Toulemonde, J. (1999). Incentives, constraints, and culture-building as instruments for the development of evaluation demand. In R. Boyle & D. Lemaire (Eds.), *Building effective evaluation capacity: Lessons from practice.* New Brunswick, NJ: Transaction Publishers.

Zall, K. J., & Rist, R. C. (2004). *Un manual para profesionales del desarrollo: Diez pasos hacia un sistema de seguimiento y evaluación basado en resultados.* Washington, DC: World Bank.

Zaltsman, A. (2006a). Credibilidad y utilidad de los sistemas de monitoreo y evaluación para la toma de decisiones: Reflexiones en base a experiencias Latinoamericanas. In M. Vera (Ed.), *Evaluación para el desarrollo social: Aportes para un debate abierto en América Latina.* Guatemala City, Guatemala: MagnaTerra Publishers.

Zaltsman, A. (2006b). *Experience with institutionalizing monitoring and evaluation systems in five Latin American countries: Argentina, Chile, Colombia, Costa Rica and Uruguay.* Independent Evaluation Group ECD (Working Paper No. 16). Washington, DC: World Bank.

Zaltsman, A. (2007). *The role of monitoring and evaluation in the budgetary process: Insights from a study of Chile's performance-based budgeting system* (Dissertation submitted in partial fulfillment of the requirements for the degree of Doctor of Philosophy). Robert F. Wagner Graduate School of Public Service, New York University, New York.

NURIA CUNILL-GRAU *is senior lecturer at Centro de Investigación Sociedad y Políticas Públicas, Universidad de Los Lagos, and associate lecturer at Escuela de Salud Pública, Universidad de Chile.*

SONIA M. OSPINA *is a professor at the Wagner Graduate School of Public Service, New York University.*

NEW DIRECTIONS FOR EVALUATION • DOI: 10.1002/ev

Rotondo, E. (2012). Lessons learned from evaluation capacity building. In S. Kushner &
E. Rotondo (Eds.), *Evaluation voices from Latin America. New Directions for Evaluation,
134*, 93–101.

8

Lessons Learned From Evaluation Capacity Building

Emma Rotondo

Abstract

*This chapter shares lessons learned from evaluation capacity-building efforts
undertaken by PREVAL in recent years (2004–2010). The author also discusses
the aim of capacity building in evaluation within PREVAL, the key elements that
should be considered in planning, monitoring, and evaluation (PME) systems,
and the strategic uses of its processes and findings. Finally, the chapter outlines
lessons learned regarding the role of stakeholders, and factors for success and
failure identified from PREVAL's experience in building evaluation capacity in
antipoverty rural projects in Latin America and the Caribbean. ©Wiley Periodicals, Inc., and the American Evaluation Association.*

Resumen

*Este artículo comparte las lecciones aprendidas del desarrollo de la capacidad
de evaluación llevadas a cabo por PREVAL en los últimos años (2004–2010).
También reflexiona acerca de los elementos clave que deben ser considerados en
los sistemas de Planificación, Seguimiento y Evaluación (PME), y el uso
estratégico de sus procesos y resultados. Por último, el documento se describe
las lecciones aprendidas con respecto al rol de los actores y factores de éxito y
fracaso de los mismos, provenientes de la experiencia de PREVAL en la construcción de la capacidad de evaluación en los proyectos de lucha contra la*

pobreza rural en América Latina y el Caribe. ©Wiley Periodicals, Inc., and the American Evaluation Association.

Governments across Latin America are developing an interest in the use of planning, monitoring, and evaluation (PME) systems as a strategic information tool for public management and policy, and one consequence is energy being put into evaluation capacity development. A review of the literature on the significance of PME systems in Latin America showed the significance of PME, in particular the pioneering study by Cunill-Grau and Ospina Bozzi (2008).

The common aim is to develop and allocate resources based on the effectiveness of services and outcomes of national development plans, frequently on evidence of what works. PME is also expected to yield evidence on the gains achieved by development interventions and how this translates into improvements in people's living conditions. Though governments in the region acknowledge that accountability is an important purpose of monitoring and evaluation (M&E), there are few examples of the inclusion of citizens in the accountability frame, or as users of evaluation. This chapter presents a case of institutional capacity development for PME and for participatory approaches by focusing on the PREVAL network.

What Is PREVAL?

The Regional Platform for Evaluation Capacity Building in Latin America and the Caribbean (PREVAL) seeks to enhance efficiency and effectiveness in rural development programs, through strengthening PME systems at local and decentralized levels. PREVAL seeks to ensure that principal actors are involved in designing and implementing M&E systems (government managers, communities, and government evaluation units). Its services, to programs, evaluators, government, and rural agencies, focus on the following dimensions:

Participatory evaluation
Baseline studies, and outcome, impact evaluations
Systematization of good practice in PME
Innovative, image-based evaluation methods
Self-appraisals and organizational capacity-building plans in PME

Services are provided through meetings and workshops, internships, real-time and virtual technical support, and coordinating the support of national and regional experts. In addition, PREVAL has technical and information resources such as learning communities, a network of experts in PME, an electronic network with more than 4,000 members, and a Web platform (www.PREVAL.org) featuring relevant literature, forums, newsletters, and useful links on issues facing M&E for rural development programs.

Participatory and Learning-Oriented Evaluation Approach

The focus of PREVAL is local learning, designed for the sustainability of interventions. The ideal is that evaluation can be based on negotiation and consensus across stakeholder groups, in order to achieve shared responsibility for interventions. Participation in evaluation is thus not only about involving or consulting with citizens, but engaging them in program decision making.

Participatory evaluation provides procedures, tools, and methodologies attuned to local cultures (IFAD, 2002). It involves the development of capacities and skills guided by the following principles:

1. A joint image for preferred futures
2. Empathy expressed as a willingness to listen to others and recognize others' points of view and concerns
3. Tolerance for creativity in seeking appropriate questions and knowledge
4. Distributed leadership
5. The development of judgment in solving and preventing conflict
6. Shared responsibility for entering into commitments and decision making

This procedural approach helps to gear development interventions toward a demand-led rather than a service-led approach, shifting responsibility to communities to lead decision making concerning their own development, with government and nongovernmental agencies providing facilitation and support, that is, conceptualizing a *responsive* approach to the design of interventions.

What Roles Should Stakeholders Play in PME?

The different stakeholder roles in PME as well as the particular capacities of each are essential for identifying and feeding training and capacity-building strategies. Stakeholders play evaluation roles, bringing critical capacities to bear as appropriate. For instance, in the PREVAL framework an evaluator specializing in capacity building for groups and organizations may play a role as facilitator, trainer, or adviser in M&E processes. As a *facilitator* they will stimulate interactive processes and create enabling conditions and environments to encourage learning and knowledge creation; in a *trainer* role they will provide experience and know-how through didactic processes based on constructivist approaches and with the use of appreciative inquiry methods. Finally, as an *adviser* they will provide technical assistance on a temporary basis, to help in developing outputs and/or solving problems based on his/her expertise and qualification. These roles are often played in an interconnected manner, but it can be seen that evaluation involves an engaged and interactive process, unlike that of the external critical observer.

The professional backgrounds of evaluators and the competences available in the supply of technical services in Latin America remain variable. It is worth noting that the development of evaluation capacity is a part of the evaluation profession, with important links to education, as well as social and organizational learning, and that professional standards in this area have not yet been established in the Latin American community of evaluators. However, knowledge and skills increasingly considered to be part of the competencies of M&E experts are

1. Facilitation, coaching, and social learning knowledge and skills
2. Knowledge of social sciences research methods
3. Communication and negotiating skills (interpersonal relations)
4. Critical thinking, self-critical attitude, ethical behavior

A working group convened by PREVAL (PREVAL, 2007a, 2007b) discussed ideal roles for each of the stakeholders, in reply to the question, *what are the following stakeholders expected to do to contribute to monitoring and evaluation processes?* Table 8.1 summarizes the responses.

Lessons Learned to Institutionalize PME Systems

Key Factors and Successful Dimensions

Although demand is increasing for governmental PME systems, views differ on what constitutes the key to success—that is, what makes these systems work effectively for timely decision making and for informing citizens at several levels (Feinstein, 1993; Khan, 2003). Regional and global experiences show that PME systems work best when they combine at least three dimensions: (1) an appropriate institutional/organizational framework sensitive to critique and stakeholder engagement; (2) high-quality data to understand results and impacts; and (3) a strategy to use and communicate results so they are fed into decision making and an informed citizenry. These three elements can enable PME systems to become institutionalized while enabling understanding of these changes and engagement of the actors involved in developing negotiated solutions.

Research conducted in the region shows that context affects the organizational consistency of these systems as well as (more indirectly) the extent to which they are institutionalized—there is a considerable variability in the quality and effectiveness of PME systems (Feinstein, 2002). Research also shows that the demand for information produced by PME systems can ensure that they become institutionalized (i.e., utilized in government decision making), but that this demand needs to be created and sustained. There is also a need to raise awareness among political and administrative elites

Table 8.1. Stakeholder Contributions to PME

	Stakeholders' Roles		
M&E Steps	Community	Project Technical Unit	Government Body
Design and planning	Visualizes expected changes Participates in local M&E Calls for and encourages equitable involvement with a gender approach	Provides support and advises on self-evaluation on M&E capacity both within communities and its own organization Facilitates the development of a M&E system based on the needs and uses of communities Provides technical guidance for developing M&E Conducts dialogue, negotiates, and involves both the community and its own organization in the development of M&E Is actively involved in the development of a M&E system Drafts terms of reference for baseline studies and other outputs	Provides support to the project technical unit in implementing participatory M&E Allocates (human and financial) resources and equipment for M&E Identifies M&E capacity within its own organization Defines roles and devolves responsibilities in M&E Participates in the development of a M&E system, including the drafting of terms of reference
Implementation	Participates in data collection and takes on commitments Observes, measures, and documents any significant changes resulting from the project Is actively involved in discussing the project outcomes and impact	Facilitates processes involving the collection and analysis of evidence on change, both its own and others' Provides training and support to stakeholders in practice Consolidates and documents in a systematic manner information on project outcomes and impact, and environment	Requests and analyzes information on findings Takes part in the process of developing a M&E plan Secures timely resources for M&E Promotes learning environments and processes Institutionalizes results-based management

(Continued)

Table 8.1. (Continued)

M&E Steps	Stakeholders' Roles		
	Community	Project Technical Unit	Government Body
		Submits reports adjusted to each audience Promotes learning environments and processes Encourages participation and inspires stakeholders Provides tools for use and communication of findings	Fosters a suitable organizational climate for participatory management and learning
Use of outputs	Uses data for suggesting solutions and guiding strategies Shares and communicates findings Opens up spaces for dialogue and reflection on change	Uses data for suggesting solutions and guiding/redirecting actions Communicates findings to different stakeholders Promotes the use of information for improving both its own organizational practice and that of communities Influences decision makers Opens up spaces for dialogue and reflection	Uses data for decision making and policy making Reports to citizens on findings Promotes the use of data produced as a result of M&E Promotes institutionalization of best practice and learning obtained as a result of M&E

regarding the value of PMEs for achieving impact and the need to invest in measurements, throughout the project implementation cycle.

The Role of PME Systems

Experience shows, as suggested above, that the roles and functions of PME should adjust to the needs, uses, and decision-making processes of multiple stakeholders, rather than project management only—in fact, stakeholders can play a role in evaluation processes, making contributions according to their capacities (Patton, 2004). This brings benefits and advantages beyond the enhancement of decision making, in terms of improved governance and citizen awareness.

When key stakeholders in a development intervention make their own decisions regarding change and have access to resources and opportunities for organizing themselves, they develop capabilities and knowledge that are a source of empowerment—that is, the ability to influence the environment and achieve sustainable change. A structural source of exclusion is precisely powerlessness. One element in poverty reduction is the enhancement of citizen/stakeholder agency and the redistribution of power in the context of development projects. One implication of this is that competences offered by the supply of technical M&E services need to be adjusted to the needs of diverse stakeholder and citizen groups, rather than just formal project teams. Evaluators need to be theorists of empowerment.

M&E Capacity Development

The experience of rural development projects in the Latin American region shows that success is built upon *social capital*, that is, the development of an infrastructure of knowledge and capacity that can embrace and sustain changes that have agreed-upon public value. To promote a culture of consensus and develop social capital in these terms, new M&E approaches insist on actions leading to

- Decentralized decision making to open up opportunities for local development
- Increasing reliance on local technical talent
- Distributed leaderships and teamwork
- An agreed-upon vision for the future that attaches value to cultural and gender-based identity
- Information networks including those based on new technologies to enhance direct access to wide markets
- An environment seen as enabling so that community, social, producers, and marketing organizations mobilize and manage resources in a more independent and confident manner

Conclusions

Based on this discussion, I offer four main conclusions.

1. Participatory assessment methodologies are historically and widely used in the region, especially in programs and projects at local level and in the context of PME systems, Citizens Observatories, and even in research and development of rural innovations.
2. There is a broad application of participatory methods of evaluation oriented to social learning. The region shows a variety of methodologies, coming mainly from civil society organizations and projects (Ballón et al., 2004; Douthwaite et al., 2007; Horton et al., 2011; Pasteur & Blauert, 2004).
3. However, in recent years external evaluations of public programs and projects and international cooperation have been turning the focus toward determining the impact of performance and results, omitting participation as a value (Aedo, 2005; Baker, 2000; Grupo Interagencial de Desarrollo Rural, 2009).
4. The regional debate on approaches and standards of evaluation is in its beginnings. The regional community of evaluation—the Latin America Network for Monitoring and Evaluation, ReLAC, its members, and institutions such as PREVAL and other capacity-building programs debate widely on approaches to evaluate social programs that seek inclusion and equity.

References

Aedo, C. (2005). *Evaluación de impacto*. Santiago de Chile, Chile: CEPAL, División de Desarrollo Económico.

Baker, J. (2000). *Evaluación del impacto de proyectos de lucha contra la pobreza. Manual para profesionales*. Washington, DC: Banco Internacional de Reconstrucción y Fomento/Banco Mundial.

Ballón, E., Brackelaire, V., De Zutter, P., Molano, O. L., Monge, C., Perret, H., & Piña, J. (2004). *Impacto en la reducción de la pobreza rural: Cuatro experiencias ilustrativas*. Lima, Perú: PREVAL and IFAD.

Cunill-Grau, N., & Ospina Bozzi, S. M. (2008). *Fortalecimiento de los sistemas de monitoreo y evaluación (M&E) en América Latina. Comparative report of 12 countries*. Caracas, Venezuela: Centro Latinoamericano de Administración para el Desarrollo, CLAD and Banco Mundial.

Douthwaite, B., Alvarez, S., Cook, S., Davies, R., George, P., Howell, J., . . . Rubiano, J. (2007). Participatory impact pathways analysis: A practical application of program theory in research-for-development. *Canadian Journal of Program Evaluation, 22*(2), 127–159.

Feinstein, O. (1993). *Focused rapid assessment of monitoring and evaluation systems (FRAME)* (Report No. 0449). Rome, Italy: Monitoring and Evaluation Division, Economic and Planning Department, IFAD.

Feinstein, O. (2002). Use of evaluations and evaluation of their use. *Evaluation, 8*(4), 433–439.

Horton, D., Oros, R., Ybarnegaray, R. P., Lopez, G., Velasco, C., Rodriguez, F., . . . Thiele, G. (2011). *The participatory market chain approach: Experiences and results in four Andean cases* (CIP Social Sciences Working Paper 2011–1).

IFAD. (2002). *Managing for impact in rural development. A guide for project monitoring and evaluation*. Rome, Italy: IFAD.

Khan, K. (2003). *Strengthening of monitoring and evaluation systems*. Islamabad, Pakistan.

Pasteur, K., & Blauert, J. (2004). Seguimiento y evaluación participativos en América Latina: Panorama bibliográfico y bibliografía anotada. Lima, Perú: PREVAL.

Patton, M. Q. (2004, October). Utilization-focused evaluation. Keynote address. In *First ReLAC Conference on Evaluation, Democracy and Governance: Challenges Facing Latin America and the Caribbean*, Lima, Perú.

PREVAL. (2005). *III. Síntesis del taller de entrenamiento e intercambio de consultores* [Summary of a training and exchange workshop for PREVAL consultants, internal document]. Lima, Perú: Author.

PREVAL. (2007a). *Concept note on a capacity-development guide in monitoring and evaluation*. Lima, Perú: Author.

PREVAL. (2007b). *Report on a seminar on local capacity building with partners in monitoring and evaluation for rural development*. Lima, Perú: Author.

RIOPLUS/GTZ Honduras. (2004). *Sondeo a unidades de planificación y evaluación de gestión (UPEG)* (internal document). Tegucigalpa, Honduras: Rio Plus.

EMMA ROTONDO is a social anthropologist, facilitator, and coach, works in evaluation capacity building, is PREVAL executive director (www.preval.org), and is a founding member of EvalPeru/ReLAC.

NEW DIRECTIONS FOR EVALUATION • DOI: 10.1002/ev

Feinstein, O. N. (2012). Evaluation as a learning tool. In S. Kushner & E. Rotondo (Eds.),
Evaluation voices from Latin America. New Directions for Evaluation, 134, 103–112.

9

Evaluation as a Learning Tool

Osvaldo Néstor Feinstein

Abstract

Evaluation of programs or projects is often perceived as a threat. This is to a great extent related to the anticipated use of evaluation for accountability, which is often prioritized at the expense of using evaluation as a learning tool. Frequently it is argued that there is a trade-off between these two evaluation functions. An alternative approach is that accountability complements the role of evaluation as a learning tool, as accountability provides an incentive for learning. This complementarity between learning and accountability is facilitated by the development of an evaluation culture where mistakes are seen as opportunities for learning and learning as an important source for growth and development. © Wiley Periodicals, Inc., and the American Evaluation Association.

Resumen

Con frecuencia la evaluación de los programas o proyectos se percibe como una amenaza. En gran medida esto está relacionado con el uso previsto de evaluación para la rendición de cuentas, que a menudo es priorizado a expensas de utilizar la evaluación como una herramienta de aprendizaje. Se argumenta que existe una compensación (trade-off) entre estas dos funciones de evaluación. Un enfoque alternativo es que la rendición de cuentas complementa la función de la evaluación como una herramienta de aprendizaje, puesto que la rendición de cuentas constituye un incentivo para el aprendizaje. Esta complementariedad entre la aprendizaje y rendición de cuentas se ve facilitado por el desarrollo de una cultura de evaluación, donde los errores son vistos como oportunidades para aprender, y los aprendizajes como una importante fuente de crecimiento y desarrollo. © Wiley Periodicals, Inc., and the American Evaluation Association.

Perception of Evaluation as a Threat

The potential danger that programs, projects, or policies might be disrupted or discontinued as a result of evaluations, or that the professional careers of those involved in the management or implementation of interventions being subject to evaluation could be negatively affected, has led to a defensive attitude toward evaluation. People often try to avoid evaluations by postponing their starting date, trying to show that evaluations are either unnecessary or untimely (because everything that has to be known is already known), or claiming that activities still need to be completed or not all the data required are available. These concerns are all the more frequent where resources available to continue programs are scarce and people are afraid that an evaluation might endanger their opportunities.

The above situation regards evaluation as an instrument for accountability only. Though this is indeed one of the roles of evaluation, evaluation has a further role to promote learning from experience. This emphasis on learning and improving interventions may help in changing perceptions of evaluation. But it has also sometimes led to evaluations leaving aside their role as an instrument for accountability, thus shifting the pendulum from one extreme to the other.

Relationship Between the Accountability and Learning Roles of Evaluation

There is a widespread view that the two roles of evaluation collide with each other and that there is a trade-off between both functions, that if the role of evaluation as a learning tool is to be prioritized then its accountability function needs to be given less weight. An alternative sees the two evaluation functions as complementary. This is not to make a virtue out of necessity. Complementarity exists where accountability provides an incentive for learning (Feinstein & Beck, 2006; Leeuw, Rist, & Sonnichsen, 1993; O'Donnell, 2007; O'Neill, 2002; Perrin, 2006; Peruzzotti & Smulovitz, 2002; Przeworski, Stokes, & Manin, 1999). In fact, accountability may involve showing that learning from experience has taken place and that if mistakes were made this was because there were no relevant antecedents. Mistakes may be considered part of the cost of the learning process. It is interesting to note that accountability has been translated into Spanish as *responsabilización* and *responsabilizarse*—to make oneself responsible. The alternative expression, *rendición de cuentas* draws attention to *cuentas* (accounts).

On the other hand, if progress toward achievement of the intervention's objectives is not accounted for, the potential for learning from experience

Table 9.1. Relations Between Learning and Accountability

	Learning by	Accountability to
Who?	Civil society	Civil society
	Government(s) donors	Government(s) donors
What?	What worked (and did not work)	Use of funds
	Lessons learned	Quality of interventions
When?	During implementation	During implementation
	Following implementation	Following implementation
How?	Diverse methodologies	Evaluations by objectives
		Social and traditional audits

will be limited. In fact, being aware of which objectives were achieved, and which were not, and the different levels at which they were achieved, will help in identifying practices that could be eventually replicated in similar contexts or which would not merit generalization.

Some international organizations, such as the International Fund for Agricultural Development (IFAD) and the World Bank (WB), demand that program or project proposals include a section on lessons learned, and clarify how these lessons were taken into consideration in proposals for new operations. Experience with implementation of this rule has shown that it can make designers of new operations aware of the learning drawn by the organization as a result of evaluations and facilitate the process of reviewing operations to ensure that experience is effectively considered; and puts pressure on (thus working as an incentive for) those designing new operations to incorporate learning, so as to avoid criticism during the process of approval.

In order to shed light on relations between learning and accountability we might consider the following essential questions, which are elaborated on in Table 9.1.

1. Who does the learning and to whom is he or she accountable?
2. What is learned and what is (or should be) accounted for?
3. When does learning take place and when should accountability take place?
4. How does/should learning take place and how should accountability take place?

Understanding the complementarity of the learning and accountability functions will help in overcoming the view that evaluation is a threat. However, this understanding is not enough to change perceptions and create a more positive attitude towards evaluation. The following sections will therefore try to make a contribution in this direction.

The Importance of Learning From Experience

Difficulties involved in this type of learning can be illustrated by the following two conflicting statements: (a) history does not repeat itself, and (b) those who cannot learn from history are doomed to repeat it. The first statement suggests that context overwhelms generalization and that making analogies between different situations is fruitless. At the extreme, this risks a nihilist approach to learning from experience. The second statement refers to the costs of failing to learn from experience, and hence the potential for repeating error. But generalizing from history is complex, and wrong lessons may also be drawn. The risk in this position, which emphasizes the need to develop an understanding of history, is that it can lead to a naiveté in the use of history, and a dismissal of the particularities of context. The challenge is to navigate between the Scilla (or rock) of nihilism and the Charybdis (or hard place) of naiveté. No two situations are exactly alike, nor are they necessarily entirely different, a paradox at the heart of evaluation.

Bandura (1982) looks at vicarious social learning, that is, generalizing from the experience of others. In neoinstitutional economic terms, one of the most severe difficulties in learning from experience is path dependence, a sort of inertia. Evaluation can be an instrument to reduce inertia by validating alternatives.

How Does Evaluation Allow Learning From Experience?

If plans and intentions were always fulfilled and there were no undesired outcomes, evaluation would cease to be useful, other than for confirmation. This type of world would harbor no uncertainties; ex ante would coincide with ex post. But in the real world plans are not always fulfilled, or only partially fulfilled, and often yield unexpected outcomes, positive and negative. One of the functions of evaluation is to address the complexities of attribution. The articulation of process-based and outcomes-focused evaluations is one strategy for dealing with the uncertainties of attribution.

Evaluation can and should help avoid the strongest risk faced by those wishing to learn from experience: the post hoc ergo propter hoc fallacy where causality is confused with sequentiality. For example, if a rural development project was implemented in a region of a country and the income of the rural population in that region showed an increase, this does not necessarily mean that the increase in income was a result of the project, because this positive outcome could be due, for instance, to a spontaneous increase in prices of produce. Here lies the value of evaluation in documenting context, counterfactuals and alternative explanations (Feinstein, 1998; Pawson & Tilley, 1997).

Evaluation Criteria

Evaluation requires a systematic consideration of principles and criteria: relevance of the object to be evaluated, effectiveness (the extent to which objectives were achieved), and efficiency (in using the right means for achieving objectives). Sometimes sustainability of results, institutional development, and coherence of programs or projects are also considered evaluation criteria. However, sustainability can be considered a part of effectiveness (if results are not sustainable, then effectiveness will be limited to the short term), whereas institutional development can be either an objective or an unintended outcome. Coherence can be considered a part of the relevance of the intervention (policy, program, or project). Applying Occam's razor, evaluation criteria could be limited to the three criteria mentioned above (Feinstein, 2007).

An intervention's relevance is established by linking its objectives to the strategy of the country, sector, organization, or institution that designed the intervention. An evaluation, therefore (unlike an audit) regards an intervention's objectives as data and it assesses them. For example, it may be that a project objective was to build a road connecting two cities and that this objective was achieved in an efficient manner, but this road was not a priority, as there already was an alternative road, whereas the human development strategy of the country attached special significance to health-care improvement in rural areas through the creation of community health-care centers. In this case, the relevance of the intervention would in principle be limited by context.

Effectiveness is taken as the extent to which an intervention's objectives are achieved. As mentioned earlier, if the objectives consider a timeline that is not limited to the short term, judgment on effectiveness should include sustainability of the intervention results. Sustainability of an intervention is often confused with sustainability of the intervention's results, and the development evaluation literature includes a significant number of references pointing to the nonsustainability of project implementation units, as well as seemingly logical recommendations such as not to include this type of unit in the design of interventions. In fact, what should really matter is sustainability of results, and in some contexts (such as in economies lacking solid structures either as a result of natural disasters or because they are undergoing the first phase of a transition towards a different type of system, or the cases of fragile states) project implementation units could play an important role as the scaffolds of further program construction. Just as it would make no sense for a scaffold to continue to be in place once a construction is completed, the same principle would apply to implementation units once the expected results (which may include building organizational capacity) have been achieved.

The third evaluation criterion is efficiency. If a project contributed to a relevant result but at high cost, then evaluation should highlight this. There may be other, more efficient ways of achieving the same results, or other purposes to which resources might be allocated. There are different ways of measuring efficiency, and several of them are different versions of cost–benefit analysis. What is important is to link achievements to the means used to achieve them, and to develop to the extent possible measures that can be compared against others used for measuring real or potential uses of the same amount and type of resources, benchmarking whenever possible and making suitable comparisons.

The Issue of Attribution and Ways to Address It

It is essential for evaluation to show where several program-determining factors are operating simultaneously and successively in the real world, as part of a complex reality, and that causality is most often multiple and dynamic. To take an example, a microcredit project targeted at rural beneficiaries may be one of several running at the same time. There may be additional variables, such as weather-related factors or policies affecting the prices of borrowers' inputs and/or products and therefore the revenues from their activities and their ability to repay loans.

In this context, the evaluation challenge includes four associated questions:

1. How can the effect of intervention X on key variables be identified?
2. How can this effect be isolated or differentiated from those resulting from other factors?
3. What would have happened if intervention X had not taken place (the counterfactual)?
4. What was it assumed would have happened if intervention X had not taken place?

The essential question is: What would have happened if intervention X had not taken place? Assumptions are frequently made, either implicitly or explicitly, regarding what would have happened if an intervention had not taken place, that is, the implicit or explicit counterfactual (Elster, 2006).

The first two questions require analysis—separating outcomes and identifying causes, which sometimes (particularly when evaluating international aid) tends to be considered either not feasible or of academic interest only, and it is often suggested that rather than focusing on and being concerned with attribution of results to certain interventions, one should establish the contribution of specific interventions to results. However, this does not solve, but rather shifts the problem, as it demands identification of the contribution by differentiating it from the contribution to other outcomes. So the problem remains. How can it be addressed?

One way is by using control groups, based on an evaluation design that allows drawing comparisons between two groups, one comprising those targeted by the intervention and the other comprising people who only differ from the first group in that they were not affected by the intervention (see, for example, Weiss, 1998). If a control group can be established it would allow comparisons to be drawn or differences to be established before and after the intervention, and between those who were and were not affected by the intervention. We would then have four situations, both before and after the intervention and with and without the intervention.

If a comparison is drawn between conditions before (CB) and after (CA) an intervention and it is restricted to the population group targeted by the intervention, CA/CB, this will not allow taking into account the effect of other factors. On the other hand, if differences CB/CA and the ratio of the differences corresponding to the group without the intervention before and after it, that is, WB/WA are considered jointly, changes before and after the intervention for the group affected by the intervention could be compared against changes before and after the intervention for the group not affected by the intervention.

As an example, we could take a situation where the variable measured is the average income of a group prior to a microcredit project. In this example, if the situations of the target group before and after the intervention were compared and it turned out that there had not been any change in income, this could be interpreted as the project having failed. However, if this were compared against a control group, it could emerge that, if the project had not taken place, income would have dropped by 20%, falling from, say, 100 to 80 monetary units. Conversely, if the target group's income showed an increase of 20%, and the control group's income showed an increase of 40%, what would appear to be a success would actually be a failure. Appearances may be misleading (Feinstein, 1997; Feinstein, 2007).

The question that arises immediately is whether it is feasible from a practical point of view to conduct evaluations with control groups in a development context. In some situations, and for certain types of interventions, it is indeed possible and advisable. But there are also several important situations in which this approach cannot be used.

The types of interventions in which control groups are feasible and advisable are specific (standardized) interventions that are not subject to change during implementation and are targeted at a population subgroup. In some cases evaluations are implemented by using randomized procedures or lotteries as a way to allocate scarce resources, a procedure that is often well received by the target population as a transparent way to allocate resources. These situations are particularly favorable for conducting evaluations that use control groups (see, for example, research studies quoted by Pitman, Feinstein, & Ingram, 2005, and Weiss, 1998).

But randomized evaluations are not feasible for evaluations on global policy issues, or monetary policy, or projects or programs in which interventions are subject to significant change during implementation, or national programs targeted at the entire population, which do not allow randomization as a procedure for allocating resources.

There may, in addition, be a number of plausible, competing hypotheses for explaining results achieved (or not achieved), such as the effect of prices not influenced by the intervention, or migration, or other external factors, including other interventions. One of the major challenges facing evaluators is identifying those plausible rival hypotheses and to consider to what extent they can be eliminated. One useful way of doing this is conducting a comparative study where comparisons are drawn against situations where the same external factors played a role, even if using a "control group" is not possible. It is worth mentioning that an important aspect of the development experience of China involves experimenting with different production and distribution systems, including different technologies; through a nonformal evaluation process those experiments that yielded better results are identified and replicated at a larger scale in the rest of the country, thereby disseminating the learning results.

Difficulties and Ways Forward

There are a number of main difficulties preventing evaluation from being used as a learning tool, each requiring a different strategy for overcoming the particular difficulty.

Not Enough Funding

Although this is generally true, funds earmarked for evaluation (allocating for example, between 1 and 2% of intervention funds for evaluation) are frequently either not used or are reallocated for other purposes.

Limited Capacity

There is, across the region, a gap between the demand for evaluation specialists and the existing supply. Typically, there is a lag between elaborating the practice of evaluation and the teaching of it—informed training of evaluators is to be done by those who practice it. Although there is a tradition of policy studies in Latin America in universities and policy research institutes, its extension into training for program evaluation is not yet fully accomplished (Bresser Pereira & Cunill Grau, 1999; Fukuyama, 2004).

Lack of Incentives

Where evaluations are seen as a threat, as mentioned above, this has led to evaluations sometimes being termed as "reviews" which does not resolve the issue. The problem has to do in part with the anticipated use of evaluation for accountability, which is usually emphasized at the expense of learning. In the end, the main incentives for evaluations to be conducted and to be of good quality will depend on the demand for evaluation by policy makers and the population (Ramiro Sánchez, 2002).

Conclusions

This discussion can be summarized in the following set of propositions.

The two key functions of evaluation—accountability and learning—are complementary. Evaluation, when it is well done and appropriately used, allows learning from experience, by distilling lessons on what worked and didn't work, and the reasons behind successes and failures.

Evaluation criteria (relevance, effectiveness, and efficiency) allow systematically considering (and drawing lessons from) a number of different programs, policies, or projects.

As evaluated interventions operate within a complex context, with several factors in play, it is essential to avoid taking a naïve approach to attribution, that is, one that fails to recognize the existence of other, contextual factors besides the intervention itself.

For interventions where using control groups is feasible, and ethically acceptable, particularly very specific interventions that are not subject to change during implementation and are targeted at a population subgroup, it is advisable to conduct evaluations with the use of control groups.

Where using control groups is not feasible, it is important to consider plausible rival hypotheses and use evidence to determine which hypotheses have more solid foundations. In addition, especially where attribution is of a more conjectural nature, it is important to complement results evaluations with process evaluations.

To address the lack of funding for evaluations, it is useful to consider creating a dedicated budget for evaluations, which could be a percentage of the total funding allocated for interventions (between 1 and 2%).

Training in evaluation may be complemented with the creation of hands-on learning opportunities based on the experience of evaluation practice.

Both evaluators and evaluation managers should become involved not only in the production but also the postproduction phase of evaluations, taking on responsibility for promoting the use of the evaluation findings. A division of labor with communication experts may be useful to prevent evaluations from producing evaluation reports that are shelved (or posted in a Web site) without use, and to allow them to become useful learning tools (Feinstein, 2002).

Establishing awards for best-quality or most influential evaluations can be used as an incentive for quality improvement. But the main incentives for evaluations to be used as a learning tool will depend on the demand for evaluations by policy makers and the population.

The monitoring and evaluation networks that have been established in Latin America, such as ReLAC and the Latin America and the Caribbean Monitoring and Evaluation Network, could play a more active role in promoting evaluation as a learning tool, involving civil society and governments as well as academia.

References

Bandura, A. (1982). *Social learning theory*. Madrid, Spain: Espasa Calpe.

Bresser Pereira, L. C., & Cunill Grau, N. (Eds.). (1998). *Lo público no estatal en la reforma del estado.* Buenos Aires, Argentina: Paidós.

Elster, J. (2006). *Logic and society.* Barcelona, Spain: Gedisa.

Feinstein, O. (Ed.). (1997). *Experiencias Latinoamericanas en seguimiento y evaluación.* La Paz, Bolivia: FIDA-NOGUB COSUDE.

Feinstein, O. (1998). Review of Pawson, R. & Tilley, N. Realistic evaluation. *Evaluation, 4*(2), 243–246.

Feinstein, O. (2002). Use of evaluations and the evaluation of their use. *Evaluation, 8*(4), 433–439.

Feinstein, O. (2007). *Evaluación pragmática de políticas públicas* (No. 836). Madrid, Spain: Información Comercial Española.

Feinstein, O., & Beck, T. (2006). Evaluation of development interventions and humanitarian action. In I. F. Shaw, J. C. Greene, & M. M. Mark (Eds.), *Handbook of evaluation: Policies, programs and practices.* London, England: Sage.

Fukuyama, F. (2004). *State-building.* Ithaca, NY: Cornell University Press.

Leeuw, F., Rist, R., & Sonnichsen, R. C. (1993). *Can governments learn?* New Brunswick, NJ: Transaction.

O'Donnell, G. (2007). *Disonancias.* Buenos Aires, Argentina: Prometeo.

O'Neill, O. (2002). *A question of trust.* Cambridge, England: Cambridge University Press.

Pawson, R., & Tilley, N. (1997). *Realistic evaluation.* London, England: Sage.

Perrin, B. (2006). *Moving from outputs to outcomes: Practical advice from governments around the world.* Washington, DC: The Centre for the Business of Government.

Peruzzotti, E., & Smulovitz, C. (Eds.). (2002). *Controlando la política.* Buenos Aires, Argentina: Temas.

Pitman, G. K., Feinstein, O., & Ingram, G. K. (Eds.). (2005). *Evaluating development effectiveness: Challenges and the way forward.* New Brunswick, NJ: Transaction.

Przeworski, A., Stokes, S., & Manin, B. (Eds.). (1999). *Democracy, accountability and representation.* Cambridge, England: Cambridge University Press.

Ramiro Sánchez, A. (2002). *Demandas de calidad de la administración pública: Un derecho de la ciudadanía.* Madrid, Spain: Dykinson.

Weiss, C.H. (1998). *Evaluation.* Upper Saddle River, NJ: Prentice Hall.

OSVALDO NÉSTOR FEINSTEIN *is a professor of evaluation at Universidad Complutense de Madrid and was a professor at the Latin American Faculty for the Social Sciences (FLACSO).*

INDEX

A

Abarca, H., 40, 41
Abramovich, V., 31
Accountability: characterizing Latin American education reform (2000s), 19, 20t–21; evaluation as instrument of, 3; evaluation used to institutionalize governmental results and, 77–89; M&E (monitoring and evaluation) and, 94, 95, 97t–98t, 99; PME systems function of, 78–79, 89; relationship between evaluation roles of learning and, 104–105t; *responsabilización* and *rendición de cuentas* expression of, 104
Active citizenship: examining strategic use of evaluation in, 2–3; Public Observatories (Ecuador) evaluation enhancing, 2; social observatories enhancing, 34, 89
Aedo, C., 100
Aguilar Villanueva, L. F., 9
AMAR Beneficent Association, 66
Anderson, J., 43
Anduaga, J., 1

B

Baker, J., 100
Ballón, E., 100
Bamberger, M., 79
Bandura, A., 106
Bañón, R., 11
Barrón, J. C., 22
Batliwala, S., 44
Beck, T., 104
Betting on the Future program (Brazil): background information on, 64; evaluation of the, 67–75; identified priorities of the, 65; partnership participation with, 65–66; situation analysis conducted on the, 64–65
Betting on the Future program evaluation: criteria, indicators, and instrumentation used during, 69fig; data collection sources during, 68–70; lessons learned from, 72, 73t–74t; looking for evidence of merit and impact during, 68; questions and processes of the, 67–68; results on impact and merit of program, 71; social contexts addressed during the, 67; validation process of the, 70
Blauert, J., 100
Bolsa Familia programs (Brazil), 40
Bozeman, B., 11
Brandão, D. B., 3, 49, 51, 59
Brandsen, T., 26
Brazil: evaluating the Betting on the Future program in, 64–75; evaluation of Pró-Menino Program of, 50–59; historic political and cultural development of, 63–64; intersectoral commissions created in, 87; Maringá Social Observatory in, 34; moving toward results-oriented budgets in, 86; MSE-MA (social-educative procedures) in, 50, 51–52, 54–55, 56, 57; Pluriannual

Plan of, 83, 85, 87; Presidential Goals monitoring systems of, 86; Statute on Children and Adolescents (ECA) of, 50, 55; Telefonica Foundation of, 50–51. *See also* Latin America
Bresser Pereira, L. C., 110
Buendía Eximan, L., 21

C

Campbell, D. T., 69
Campbell, T., 35
Candau, V. M., 33
Candela, A., 24
Cardenas, S., 31
Carlson, B., 24
Carrillo, E., 11
Casey, M. A., 69
Catsambas, T. T., 67
Cejudo, G. M., 9
Centro Latinoamericano de Administración para el Desarrollo (CLAD), 15
Cesgranrio Foundation (Brazil), 64, 66
Chambers, R., 1
Chianka, T., 2
Chile: intersectoral commissions created in, 87; moving toward results-oriented budgets in, 86; MPE reports in context of external evaluations, 88; PME system sustainability in, 88; Presidential Goals monitoring systems of, 86; SCG of, 84, 86, 87, 88. *See also* Latin America
Chile Solidario, 40
"Citizens Observatories," 34
Citizenship: emerging consensus on recovering, 2–3; examining strategic use of evaluation in, 2–3; Public Observatories (Ecuador) evaluation enhancing active, 2; social observatories enhancing active, 34, 89
Civil society organizations (CSOs), 50
CLAD-World Bank Project, 78
Codas, R., 3
Coleman, J., 22
Colombia (Columbia): intersectoral commissions created in, 87; PME system sustainability in, 88; PME systems and institutional coherence in, 85; SINERGIA of, 10, 83, 85, 87. *See also* Latin America
Convention 169 (ILO), 44
Convention on the Elimination of all Forms of Discrimination against Women (CEDAW), 43–44
Cook, T. D., 13
Costa Rica: intersectoral commissions created in, 87; PME systems and institutional coherence in, 85; SINE of, 83, 87. *See also* Latin America
Costa Rica—State of the Nation, 34
Council on Children and Adolescents, 57
Creemers, B.P.M., 22
Cronbach, L., 67

113

ORDER FORM SUBSCRIPTION AND SINGLE ISSUES

DISCOUNTED BACK ISSUES:

Use this form to receive 20% off all back issues of *New Directions for Evaluation*.
All single issues priced at **$23.20** (normally $29.00)

TITLE   ISSUE NO.   ISBN

_____   _____   _____

_____   _____   _____

_____   _____   _____

Call 888-378-2537 or see mailing instructions below. When calling, mention the promotional code JBNND
to receive your discount. For a complete list of issues, please visit www.josseybass.com/go/ev

SUBSCRIPTIONS: (1 YEAR, 4 ISSUES)

☐ New Order   ☐ Renewal

U.S.	☐ Individual: $89	☐ Institutional: $295
CANADA/MEXICO	☐ Individual: $89	☐ Institutional: $335
ALL OTHERS	☐ Individual: $113	☐ Institutional: $369

Call 888-378-2537 or see mailing and pricing instructions below.
Online subscriptions are available at www.onlinelibrary.wiley.com

ORDER TOTALS:

Issue / Subscription Amount: $ _____

Shipping Amount: $ _____
(for single issues only – subscription prices include shipping)

Total Amount: $ _____

SHIPPING CHARGES:

First Item $6.00
Each Add'l Item $2.00

(No sales tax for U.S. subscriptions. Canadian residents, add GST for subscription orders. Individual rate subscriptions must
be paid by personal check or credit card. Individual rate subscriptions may not be resold as library copies.)

BILLING & SHIPPING INFORMATION:

☐ **PAYMENT ENCLOSED:** *(U.S. check or money order only. All payments must be in U.S. dollars.)*

☐ **CREDIT CARD:** ☐ VISA   ☐ MC   ☐ AMEX

Card number _____ Exp. Date _____

Card Holder Name _____ Card Issue # _____

Signature _____ Day Phone _____

☐ **BILL ME:** *(U.S. institutional orders only. Purchase order required.)*

Purchase order # _____
Federal Tax ID 13559302 • GST 89102-8052

Name _____

Address _____

Phone _____ E-mail _____

Copy or detach page and send to: **John Wiley & Sons, One Montgomery Street, Suite 1200,**
San Francisco, CA 94104-4594

Order Form can also be faxed to: **888-481-2665**

PROMO JBNND